ORPHEUS

ORPHEUS AND THE MUSES
by Lucien Coutaud
a tapestry executed in 1942

ORPHEUS

A SYMPOSIUM OF THE ARTS

EDITED BY

John Lehmann

VOL : I

JOHN LEHMANN : LONDON

1948

FIRST PUBLISHED IN 1948 BY
JOHN LEHMANN LTD
MADE AND PRINTED IN GREAT BRITAIN BY
PURNELL AND SONS, LTD
PAULTON AND LONDON

Foreword

A<small>N</small> <small>EDITOR</small>, like any other showman, is sometimes stung into exclaiming to his critics, that bricks can't be made without straw, even though he may feel that he can make a very much better brick out of a judicious use of the straw available than some of his colleagues. But if, in even the finest season for straw, he presents them proudly with a newly named brick, and they find that the straw is not after all very different and ask him why he has changed the name, they may justly expect a reasoned explanation. Why, they may in fact ask, call your production *Orpheus* when so much of the taste and so many of the contributors are the same as we found in *New Writing and Daylight*?

The easy way for anyone, in any job that involves the presentation of the creative work of others, is, once he has found a successful formula, to stick to it through all the years he remains responsible, ignore both the triumphs and failures of those who try other formulas, and avoid at least the charges of inconsistency—or even treachery—that the most habit-forming of his fans will level at him if he begins to change direction.

There is, however, another way which seems to me more honourable and more creative. If an editor is to have any success, he almost certainly needs to have some conception about what literature, what art in the most general sense of the word means and can do, which is shared by his contemporaries, or which he can gradually persuade them to share because it has existed unformulated just below the conscious level of their thinking for some time. That seems to me the fundamental quality, the X that an Editor must possess if he sets out to do more than mark off a dumping ground for the surplus production of typewriters; but the way he presents that X, and what he associates it with, is likely to vary according to the particular circumstances of the time when he starts his venture.

Such circumstances do not have to be, altogether or even predominantly political and economic, but are to a great extent of the deeper mind whose tidal movements have often only the most obscure and indirect relation to immediately fashionable political ideals or day to day events in history. As the tide moves, the circumstances change; this is always happening, sometimes slower, sometimes faster; and if an editor remains unaware of them, or ignores them for reasons of narrow security, he is likely to cease very soon to be able to provide any creative release or stimulus to living art. He should, I believe, be hyper-sensitively aware of these movements and changes, and alter his formula as often as the movement is appreciable, alter his balance of material, alter what he asks his contributors to do, alter his format and material presentation, and finally, when the change has gone so far that the original purpose seems almost out of sight, make a clean break and alter the name. But at the same time something essential, I believe, should remain: all these alterations, these changes of accent of flavour, will have little creative value unless X is present in every variation, to provide the basic cohesive force. How it manifests itself will probably not be very easy to define, even for the editor himself; but one way will almost certainly be his continuing choice of certain outstanding contributors.

It is because I have been aware that the formula which made the original *New Writing*, and was varied again when it became *New Writing and Daylight*, has been gradually changing, and because I wanted to take that change even further, that I decided on an altogether new title. Not only is it less confusing as well as more honest, but it also gives us the opportunity to re-design the whole book, to make it typographically more pleasing, more richly embellished and more adequately illustrated.

In criticism and appreciation *Orpheus* will be concerned not only with literature but with all the arts—at least potentially. There are admirable magazines devoted to literature, or drama, or painting, or music separately; there should be more where they can all come together in a *Festspiel* of the printed page, proclaiming their kinship by proof and lighting one another with interlinked fires. In the search for what is adventurous in thought or imagination, *Orpheus* will know no national boundaries, but will everywhere choose what is visionary rather than what is merely realistic, what rejects the dogmas and what looks at truth everyday with fresh eyes. *Orpheus* will, in particular, listen to those poets, or painters, or other artists who are speaking about their own art.

The deep need today is to assert the lyrical and imaginative spirit against materialism and the pseudo-sciences; this is not new, for it is precisely what Shelley and other great creative minds of his time were proclaiming one hundred and fifty years ago, but it is even more urgent in our own lives upon which the same dangers can act so much more frightfully and more swiftly. Nor is it new that it should be equally urgent to assert the rights and dignity of the individual human being against the pretensions of the state; it is one of the oldest of wars, but the enemy has returned to the offensive armed with far greater powers than the spies of the Inquisition ever knew, and the encroaching sahara of his *paperasserie* is far vaster and more chokingly arid. The terrors of the world we live in have bred their own anti-humanism, putting despair and cynicism on a pedestal of the latest philosophical fashions; but such anti-humanism is just as much the enemy as the belief in the absolute state or in salvation by political means alone, or in finding the solution to the mystery of life by the study of comparative cycles of history or conditioned reflexes in animals. That is why it seems to me so important to say quietly but firmly that the poet is the creator, and the word of the poet is the mainspring of history; that all the devilish things that menace us are the invention of those who need an ounce of civet to sweeten their imagination—and that only the poet can provide it; and to go on saying it and to make it possible for others to say it, explicitly and implicitly, in as many ways as they can.

JOHN LEHMANN

Contents

CONTENTS

List of Illustrations

xi

I

Terence Tiller

SUMMER IDYLL

Here on the dunes, where children's pumping feet press home
    into the tawny breasts, and rattle
the fallen bones of cliffs; before the gleam
of a great emerald-glass crawling petal,
behind the bungalows as trim and bright with paint
    as little yachts, I lie; and if I look,
the grass against them circles me, sharp and intent
    and stiff as rigging; shadows of gulls wave back.

Here in the velvet lion's-paws of sun, the purr
    of sleepy light, I rest; and hear the summer
wheel round me like my blood; and watch the fire
    —garnet, black, and gold—feel the murmur
of heat upon my lids: earth dances now; and heat,
    reeling in the bruised pebbles round me, stares
like an audience through her shining garments, her light
    melismata of lacy skirt of flowers.

In such a time, the heart erect with happiness,
    what else to think but the cool apple-blossom
flush of an early love?—how else caress
    myself upon the moment's lissome
its flesh-warmed silk; feel quivering beneath my hand
    live articulations, commerce of skin,
a lover's body pleased and flowering out of sand?
    And revisiting love haunted by the sun?

    Love naked among boughs and garlands, among
    the feather-growing cold of woods, and flushed
    with coral under honey; love with a tongue
of birds and fountains, where birds and fountains flashed

like a bowl of jewels; love simple as a hand;
   legend or pastoral: kinder than the sweet
   aching of Amaryllis, than the sound
   (through gilded groves and fields) of Daphnis' flute:

   not only gods were sure of it. For mortals,
   bright from the running and the flower-throwing,
   soft hands of air lascivious in their kirtles
   —love on the tasselled grass where spring was strewing
   the excellently shining pools of sheep,
   stood round them strong and innocent as the sun:
bodies awake as burning eyes, all else asleep:
   the love, the lovers, and the place, were one.

She, if immortal, dancing like a sunny field,
   the grass of Paradise, and poets there;
   a gentle house, unguarded as a child,
     wide as the splendour of the air.
Mortal, then rooted in what innocence, to be
    the grace and perfume of a tree,
   sweet as a lilac walking?—and her words
like jewels dropping into water, all her speech
   delicate as an eyelash or her touch
   —and fingers like the bones of little birds.

   So, like a yacht's abandonment of all self
   but the grace only, a strong and comely sail,
   they leaned on loving. Summer: the restless gulf,
   the walking in us of a masterless will:
veins running sunlight, the body one fierce hand
   of agony of love. And water beat,
drowning in brilliance, gently by us, to the sound
   (through gilded groves and fields) of Daphnis' flute.

   Tree after tree alive in leopard's clothing
   swung into curtains, and bowed us into shade
   —under whose lace of leaves the softly breathing
grass beckoned round us; and smooth and free and wide
   as doors, the wind was opened upon day.
   Oh calmly rocking sky, and the sun a fall
of angels shouting over us; love, the land at play
   —the reeling land where birds were bountiful
   and love a star in the heart, and love in the mouth
like strawberries, and the amazed flesh sensitive as a moth.

For such an amorous Arcadian space of air
   of mother-kindly air more gently turning
  than a warm infant's head, more smooth and near
    than a wife's cheek; its huge blue burning
intimate as a bed—for such a cone and pulse
   of spangled wind, the self unfolds as for
a bride; its memory trails fingers through her pearls;
  and the heart's fiction is declared like war.

Tired of the tireless rocking in a million beds,
   all birth behind her, careless now of praise,
  like an old woman, the sea smiles and nods;
    the sunlight aching in her eyes.
Lips that were once Cassandra's or the leap of wolves,
  now ineffectual as eyelids, fall
and fold and writhe and fall and lisp over themselves
  and their soft food, the shore's most glittering scroll.

P. H. Newby

TEN MILES FROM ANYWHERE

THE TWO of them, small boy and mother, had been out picking wild strawberries and were almost lost in the maze of green hedges and white lanes when the countryside began to tremble. Minute puff-balls exploded in the dust. A stiff cloud like the webbed foot of a goose was propped up behind the hawthorns and the mother's voice sounded small and precise as though she were talking in a room. A flock of sheep huddled under a tree.

The drum was being struck just behind a tight wad of trees which the small boy knew to be full of rabbits. There was a long, impressive roll which explored the hollowness beneath his feet, agitated the ash leaves and smoked off enough of the dust to tickle his nose.

'Don't be afraid. It's only thunder.'

He was not afraid until he noticed that the cloud had advanced and now had depth as well as length and breadth. It was solid, with polished sides like the hoof of a bull. From the heights a string of white fire was lowered to the horizon and immediately withdrawn. In the concussion that followed a rabbit scuttled across the lane.

'At least the rain will lay the dust.'

A shattering tattoo broke out of the air.

'Silly creature! Don't be afraid. It's only thunder.'

He held himself stiffly for fear, not looking to right or to left. They had climbed over a stile and were walking back towards the house across a wide meadow. Every step they took carried them farther and farther from the protecting hedges. The unseen drummer blinked a white eye, the mother laughed gaily, and the small boy, unable to control himself any longer, raced off for the next stile. The woodwork shook under his hand and large drops of water fell on his face. The mother was still walking slowly and with apparent unconcern, swinging the chip basket in which the wild strawberries lay. From one side to the other the sky was torn like a garment and the boy cried out with terror.

It never occurred to him to run back to his mother. On to the next stile. And there were three more after it. A colt galloped madly round its field, pausing only to rear and shake its mane as though to unseat an invisible rider. The oaks made slow despondent gestures but the long stalks of the lesser hedge plants whipped angrily at each other. The small

16

boy flung himself at the next stile as the following thunderclap overtook him.

When the woman reached the house she found the back door open and the downstairs rooms deserted. She placed the chip of wild straw-berries on the kitchen table and called the boy's name, but unenquiringly and in a dead, flat voice out of which the thunder had bullied all spirit.

She went back into the garden to make sure there were no clothes on the line. Her neighbour came out of the potting shed in his garden just as the first drops of real rain pattered on the cabbages.

'It's tempest weather,' he called out.

In the back bedroom which was the boy's own she found him lying on the bed with his face pressed into the pillow. The window framed a lead sky across which the lightning flickered, so she drew the curtains and sat down by the bed to wait. The thunder had already withdrawn and was beating over Hereford. The rain which had at first been a hundred feminine voices in the garden settled down to a steady drumming and the water butt under this very window began to cough.

'We got home just in time.'

She put out a hand and laid it on the boy's head. 'You are a little idiot to be afraid of thunder.'

Swiftly he turned his face towards her.

Shocked and dismayed she tried to embrace him but he withdrew against the wall and drew the blanket over himself.

When Grandmother came on a visit she gave up every attribute but that of having an appetite for exploration and the face of an urchin, alert and button-eyed. She had nothing in common with the old lady with whom they had once lived in the great house that stood on a hill and looked down on the docks of a great port.

'What is luck?' the boy asked the old lady.

From her he learned the word 'exploration.' She gave him a zest for the countryside which she showed to be an undiscovered continent where strangely coloured fungi grew on the roots of trees, where dry firewood in fantastic shapes, was to be dragged from the hedgerows, dead even under the canopy of living leaves; and a particular tunnel that ran under the white lane, leading from one meadow into another. This tunnel had never been constructed by human hands. Or, if it had been so made, so long ago that it had been forgotten. Nothing was to detract from the joy of discovery. Once they stole a marrow growing on a dunghill. Her high urchin voice, always just failing to close on the end of each word, told him that luck was the most important thing in the world and that neither his father nor his mother had any of it.

Who then were lucky?

She made him put his ear to the telegraph post and listen to the humming. 'The folk who speak on those wires live far off. The wires run from one great city to another great city. That is why they are lucky, because they live in great cities far away.'

She told him the names of the wild flowers. For every disease from which man suffered there was a wild herb to cure it. Some flowers, she said, had an evil influence on human beings.

There were moments of silence when he wanted to know what she was thinking.

'It's an impolite question. If I wanted you to know I should tell you.'

'Therefore' was a word she used. 'As a result—it follows that—to choose between—not to put too fine a point on it—in other words.' She once showed the boy some wild flowers that she had pressed between the pages of a book fifty years before. They were like her thoughts, dry, neat and carefully labelled. She said that she never did or said anything without reason.

Drawing her lips into a tight bud so that the hairs above her mouth darkened into a moustache.

'I know you are my grandmother, which means that you are either the mother of my father or the mother of my mother. But I don't know which.'

They were, of course, alone.

'Has your mother never told you?'

'I think you are my father's mother.'

It was almost too dark to see the colour of the wild flowers.

'See,' said the old woman, bending with some difficulty and pointing her big-jointed finger. 'If you pick one of those blue flowers your mother will be struck blind.'

The air was bitter with the smell of watercress that flourished in the dank ditch on the edge of which they were standing. Bats drew uncertain lines in the darkening air. The little flowers grew in a carpet on a round-shouldered hump.

'How can that be?' the boy asked. By bending down he could see that each small flower carried a spear of yellow in its heart.

The old woman rocked with laughter.

To the boy the sights and sounds of the summer evening brought desires that would never be satisfied. The grass was crushed under the bullock's foot but the sweetness, like the luck of which his grandmother had spoken, or the private language of men in cities—a language that the country child only heard with his ear to the telegraph post—stirred and did not assuage his new tastes. Just as she had shown him that exploration was a tunnel under the lane so she could show him flowers where, he felt sure, none had grown before. She had called them up from the sod.

'What is thunder?' he demanded as though by way of further assurance.

'A sign that nature is angry. One does well to be afraid. Some people say it is electricity. That is how it is, not what it is.'

He was satisfied but nevertheless waited until she had turned her back before he picked one of the blue flowers and put it in his pocket.

It must have been Saturday evening because when they returned to the house his father was standing in the middle of the living-room with his back to Mother. Immediately the boy was alarmed by her eyes. They seemed enormous, crowding together across the top of her face and slowly moving in lustrous drops down either side of her nose. Then he saw that they were tears shining in the lamplight.

'I told the boy,' said Grandmother in her wiry voice, 'that if he picked an eyebright his mother would be struck blind. A joke on my part. Before God and without a moment's hesitation he stooped and picked one. What have you been doing to the boy, Helen?'

Helen walked over to her son and put a hand on his shoulder. 'I'm all right, you see, my dear.'

'I don't want you to be blind.'

He was frightened by her streaming eyes and tried to break free from her powerful grasp.

'What are you crying about now?' said Grandmother. 'Have you two been quarrelling again?'

'Oh, for Christ's sake leave us alone!' said Father. Then, to the boy, 'Sit down here and write me a letter.' Showing him a piece of paper and providing him with a pencil from his breast pocket.

The boy, never having been to school, could not write, but he took the pencil and began making marks on the paper. His tongue protruded from the corner of his mouth and he was pleased to be the centre of the silence in the room. He handed the paper to his father. 'What have I written?'

The man studied the paper carefully. 'You've written, "It's going to rain tomorrow."'

Overjoyed, the boy took the paper back and continued to scribble on the other side. The following day it was discovered that the tenants of their furnished cottage had absconded during the night, taking the most valuable of the furniture with them.

The policeman came, leaned his bicycle against the privet hedge and removed his clips. Grandmother called the boy in from the garden to ask whether he had explored the house next door. Father and the policeman had gone. Mother was not to be found anywhere.

To the boy's intense pleasure he found that the house next door, which he was entering for the first time, had a cellar. He was alone. He went down the wooden steps one by one and saw, by light that came through a grating, that the cellar contained an enormous teddy-bear mounted on wheels. He threw himself so violently upon its back that the bear shot forward two or three feet; but the boy was safely mounted. He cried out to it, was the hunter, was the hunted, swore at the attacking dogs. Then, overcome by a sense of guilt, slid from its back and returned to his grandmother who was waiting in the living-room of their own house.

' Well, what did you find? '

' There's a bear. I had a ride. Is it my bear or did the gipsies leave it behind? ' He had heard his father call the absconding tenants gipsies.

Mother came in angrily. ' Now what d'you think's happened? That's the last straw. They took the toy dog. It was a copy of the late King Edward's favourite pet.'

Grandmother gave a sigh of incredulity. ' I don't know at all! Why you should take it into your head to leave such a thing with the furnishings of a place you were letting beats me. Then you ask for sympathy! '

' I could have played with the toy dog and the toy bear,' said the boy.

' It's out of all proportion,' said Grandmother, ' upsetting yourself over such a silly thing. It's out of all proportion, that's what beats me. I didn't know that the late King Edward had a toy dog.'

' He didn't. This toy dog was a copy of a real dog which belonged to the King. What grieves me is that they should have taken something that belongs to Sonny. I don't care about my own things.'

' There's no need to explain things as though I were a mental defective. I was only saying you were a fool to get hysterical about the loss of a dog, a toy dog.'

' But it's not like robbing a grown person.'

' I saw the bear,' said the boy. ' Is that mine, too? I didn't know. Can I have it out in the garden? '

' You see,' said Grandmother. ' He didn't even know he had a toy dog.'

Mother stood very quiet and still. She held herself as though it were treachery to breathe and Grandmother smiled at her calmly.

' It's a wicked thing, being jealous of a mother's love.'

' I'm a mother, too, don't forget,' said Grandmother.

When Mother went up to her room Grandmother called to the boy and said they would walk down the road to meet Father and there was such a change in her voice, such a new alertness in the atmosphere, that there was all the feeling of having taken something crisp and living between the hands, a carrot, say, and snapping it in two.

The sunshine rolled down the hillside away from them.

' What would you say to this, young man? ' She had lifted him on to a stile so that he could see across the field to where the road became visible in a fat bend once more. ' Let's creep off you and me. Let's go away, and we'll live together by the seaside. Now what d'you say to that? Every morning we'll go to the pier and make paper boats. On one we'll write America, on another we'll write China. Then we'll throw them into the water and away they'll sail. To all the countries in the world.'

' You said that if I picked that flower——'

' Ah! Perhaps I was teasing, or you didn't pick enough of them. Or maybe you've got to wait for a bit, perhaps it doesn't work immediately.'

' It's impossible! It's not true, is it? '

' Are we going to the seaside, then? '

' Now? ' The boy looked round, squinting his eyes in the brightness.

' A fine morning like this! We could walk to Harewood End and catch the train.'

' Very well.' He put his hand into hers and they set off walking down the hill, for he thought of their journey as a lucky exploration with the delight of another tunnel or a crimson fungus at the end of it. In the same way they had set out and returned with the stolen marrow. This time they met Father, pushing his bicycle up the hill and shining with perspiration. He leaned on his machine and rested.

' No, no news, nothing. Disappeared into thin air, I reckon.'

' All your wife could think about was a toy dog. It would be laughable if it wasn't so tragic. Helen never did see things in proportion. Anyway,' her grip on the boy's hand tightened, ' you're finished. And you know it. You'll not get another tenant in a hurry. Perhaps you'll see reason now. The money you sank in that furniture, well, you've said good-bye to that. Little nest egg! No, your landlord days are over and you'll have to work for your living. Scribble, scribble, scribble. I'm no enemy of books. God's my witness. Come back to your own home and your own room, for it's there waiting for you. Helen and I will find a way of living together, never fear.'

' Aren't we going to the seaside now, Grandma? '

' The seaside? ' Father took the boy's hand. ' I'll tell you what we'll do. This afternoon we'll take a basket of food and have a picnic in Primrose Wood. You'd like that, wouldn't you? '

' You'll never believe me,' said Grandmother, resting her gloved hand on the handlebar and talking as though she were divulging a secret, ' I suggested to Sonny that he and I should go away to the seaside together. So he said yes and wanted to go at once. At once, mind you!'

'Don't tell that to Helen.'

'What?'

'Don't—tell—that—to—Helen,' he shouted.

It was very silent in the beech wood where, in spite of its name, no primroses grew. Overhead the branches met and tented out the sky; underneath was the leaf drift lying on bare earth for the beeches had devastated the ground they covered. But there were one or two green glades full of spiky grass, willow-herb and moths.

They were sitting on the fallen trunk of a tree when the boy left them, touching each of the smooth trunks as he came to them, until he had passed out of range of their voices and could no longer see the sunshine where they were sitting.

'Luck!' he cried out loud. His voice echoed back from the serried trunks. A squirrel shot across the ground, was motionless at the foot of a tree and then disappeared into the upper foliage. In spite of the solemn stillness he was not afraid. Some yards farther on sunlight drifted down from a great height and trailed along the ground. The voices of the family, in enquiry and anxiety, rang through the glade. It delighted the boy to hide behind one of the boles until his grandmother drew level and then jump out in an attempt to frighten her; at the same time presenting her with a yellow, trumpet-shaped flower with red stains in its throat.

'A wicked boy to wander away like that,' she remarked, taking the flower.

'I was exploring.'

'Hallo! There you are, you scamp. What's that flower?' It was Father.

Mother joined them. 'A flower for striking grandmothers blind,' she remarked.

The morning after the picnic Father took the boy by the hand and they went into the garden. 'I want you to promise me something,' he said when they were at a distance from the house. 'I don't want you to go on any more walks with your grandmother. As much as possible I want you to keep out of her way. When she speaks to you, answer politely. But don't ask her any questions. Remember that your place is by your mother's side. You're getting a young man now.'

'Why mustn't I speak to Grandmother?'

'Because I tell you and that is good enough.'

They took their meals in silence and Grandmother went off to her room immediately the sweet was served. A bumble bee swung in through the open window and out through the door.

'Listen! You can hear the combine at Pinker's.'

There was a sound like a cotton reel being whirled on a nail.

'That must be three miles from here in a straight line.'

The house next door was locked and the key hung behind their own back door so that the boy was shut out from the large toy bear. As though by way of compensation, Mother took short walks with him once more, the first since Grandmother had arrived, and he was able to show her the coloured fungus against the tree, the tunnel under the road and invite her to listen to the voices of the lucky people with one's ear laid to the telegraph pole.

In the first place, the fungus was a foul growth. Mother said that it was a parasite living on the tree just as some human beings lived on others. The only thing to do was to knock it off—just as with human beings the only thing to do was to drive them away. She had a heavy walking stick in her hand and with its help she tried to lever the fungus off the tree.

The walking stick snapped off near the handle and Mother looked at the shaft quivering in the fungus as though it spelt evil. She made no attempt to remove it.

'Come on!' she said and, seizing the boy by the hand, marched briskly up the road in the direction of the house.

'You've left the stick,' he pointed out.

'Don't say silly things.' She noticed that she was still carrying the handle of the walking stick and, with a fierce mutter, she threw it into the ditch. 'I don't want to catch you playing about with that fungus. Don't go near it, d'you understand?'

The world was getting smaller, the forbidden areas larger.

The tunnel under the lane was built to connect one field with another. The farmer could drive his cows through there without having to make them cross the right of way. 'As if there was any traffic,' she remarked with a wry smile. The tunnel was either for that or for drainage.

And the lucky voices?

They were not voices at all. There would have to be a time when human voices stopped but these voices went on and on eternally. If he left his bed in the small hours the voices would still be whispering. It was the wind in the wires.

'Then what is luck?' he asked, but either she did not hear his question or did not know the answer for she did not reply.

He insisted.

'Luck is something that we haven't got,' she said.

'When am I going to school?'

For the first time he was not reluctant to go to bed immediately after supper. After the height of June the full moon looked in through his window and the tablet of soap on the wash-stand was a translucent pearl. The hooting of the owls was an insistent sound that seemed to stare right into his heart. From below came, first of all, the rumble of the talkers and then, later, in the bedrooms, the sound of their regular breathing. Those were the only sounds save for the humming of the telegraph wires that could be heard in the stillness of the summer night.

A board creaked and Grandmother, in a long dark gown with frosty stars sprinkled over it, was standing by the side of his bed. Her voice was warm and consoling and it seemed to give him justice in spite of his initial fear at being alone with the forbidden person; he could talk and answer her questions.

She kissed him. As the car was coming early in the morning she said there would be no other opportunity to say goodbye. At the thought of her departure the boy was filled with anguish. Even the sight of her, standing in the moonlight, standing in beautiful unreality, was enough to bring back the wonder of the lucky voices and the explorations, the discoveries they had made together.

' It's a hot night. Shall we go for one last walk together? ' she suggested.

In nothing but his pyjamas and bedroom slippers and she in her starry dressing-gown they stole down the stairs, across the living-room, lifted the latch on the back door and out into the night. On the barbed wire that bounded the garden the sheep had left some clots of wool and they gave out a soft illumination of their own. Some strands of straw that he had picked from one of the gooseberry bushes were hot and slippery with dew. He looked at his grandmother's black shadow.

' What are those birds singing? ' he whispered.

' It is only one bird. It is the nightingale.'

They went out through the white gate and crossed the road which was still soft from the sun. She told him that in the morning when he awoke she would be far away and the probability was that they would never meet again.

' No, I don't want to go to Primrose Wood,' he said in fear.

The thought of walking out of the moonlight was chilling.

But Grandmother said there was no thought of going to Primrose Wood. They followed the road for a short distance, climbed over a stile and walked, as into a sea, out into the heart of a dew-swamped field. Grandmother's stiff robe rustled and her stars winked. She told him to turn. They would see the two small houses together at the top of the hill.

Grandmother picked wild roses from the hedge and made them into a posey for him. But there were more flowers, farther on, she said.

They descended into a dark lane where the sun had baked the ruts so hard that they were painful to walk over.

Finally she showed him a bank where a crowd of white flowers were growing. Their corollas were wide open as though the moon were the sun, the nightingale the morning lark.

'If you picked one of those, your mother would die,' she said.

He picked one and touched the stamens with the tip of his tongue. Grandmother showed him where to nip the neck of the corolla, find the nectaries and taste the sweetness of the flower. He stripped the bank and held all its light in his one hand.

When he went downstairs the following morning Grandmother had gone and his mother was still alive.

'Why are you watching me in that curious way?' she asked.

Father was working up in his room. It was a fresh morning of crushed clover and cloudless skies. The air moved from room to room, the wasps bit at the honeysuckle beneath the window. There was no mistaking the new note of cheerfulness. 'Oh, you're looking for your grandmother. Well, she's gone. You're a good boy, your father and I are very pleased with you. Still, we thought we wouldn't tell you before it was all over and done with.'

'Did she go by herself?'

'She went last night, after supper, my dear. The car came. She'd got a long way to go and said she preferred to travel by night for coolness.'

After breakfast he hung around the kitchen to make sure.

'Of course she went. We kissed her goodbye. I gave her a kiss for you. She said she wouldn't come up and disturb you when you were asleep.'

She was quite insensible in her happiness. Time and time again she drove the boy, with his troubled face, to play out in the field. But she found that he was repeatedly observing her through the kitchen window or through the open door. He seemed to be watching for the symptoms of disaster.

She called him in and kissed him. 'You look as though you've been getting up to some mischief.'

Now that Grandmother had gone away the boy felt alone.

'What is death?' he suddenly asked. 'When people die what happens to them?'

She had brought in some washing from the line.

'Now what put that into your head, you silly little boy?'

'Last night Grandmother and I went for a walk in our night clothes and we picked flowers.'

' You little goose, you must have been dreaming. Your grandmother went just after you were put to bed. We saw her into the car.'

' We did, we did, we did.' He stamped his foot in petty temper. ' She told me that she was going away and showed me some flowers. She said that if I picked one of them you would die.'

She looked at him in silence. Blue shadows ran over the snowy linen.

' You were dreaming, you were dreaming,' she repeated.

They went up to his bedroom and on the washstand were a few damp dog-roses and a handful of what the country people call Stars of Bethlehem.

26

Edith Sitwell

SONG

Now that Fate is dead and gone
   And that Madness reigns alone
Still the furies shake the fires
Of their torches in the street
Of my blood . . . and still they stand
In the city's street that tires
Of the tread of Man.

Three old rag-pickers are they—
Clothed with grandeur by the light
As a Queen, but blind as Doom
Fumbling for the rag of Man
In an empty room.

Now they take the place of Fate
In whom the flames of Madness ran
Since her lidless eyes were cursed
With the world-expunging sight
Of the heart of Man.

How simple was the time of Cain
Before the latter Man-made Rain
Washed away all loss and gain
And the talk of right and wrong—
Murdered now and gone.

And the ghost of Man is red
With the sweep of the world's blood . . .
In this late equality
Would you know the ghost of Man
From the ghost of a Flea?

But still the fires of the great Spring
In the desolate fields proclaim

SONG

Eternity . . . those wild fires shout
Of Christ the New Song.

Run those fires from field to field!
I walk alone and ghostlily
Burning with Eternity's
Fires, and quench the furies' song
In flame that never tires.

C. Day Lewis

THE WOMAN ALONE

I

Take any place—this garden plot will do
Where he with mower, scythe or hook goes out
To fight the grass and lay a growing fever,
Volcanic for another, dead to me;
Meek is the ghost, a banked furnace the man.

Take any time—this autumn day will serve,
Ripe with grassed fruit, raw with departing wings,
When I, whom in my youth the season tempted
To oceanic amplitudes, bend down
And pick a rotting apple from the grass.

From every here and now a thread leads back
Through faithless seasons and devouring seas:
New blooms, dead leaves bury it not, nor combers
Break it—my life line and my clue: the same
That brought him safe out of a labyrinth.

So I, the consort of an absent mind,
The emerald lost in a green waste of time,
The castaway for whom all space is island—
To follow, find, escape, this thread in hand,
Warp myself out upon the swelling past.

2

Take any joy—the thread leads always on
To here and now: snow, silence, vertigo;
His frozen face; a woman who bewails not
Only because she fears one echoing word
May bring the avalanche about her ears.

Take any joy that was—here it remains,
Corruptless, irrecoverable, cold
As a dead smile, beneath the cruel glacier
That moved upon our kisses, lambs and leaves,
Stilled them, but will not let their forms dissolve.

O tomb transparent of my waxen joys!
O lifelike dead under the skin of ice!
O frozen face of love where my one treasure
Is locked, and the key lost! May I not share
Even the bare oblivion of your fate?

But dare I throw the past into one fire,
One burning cry to break the silence, break
The cataleptic snows, the dream of falling?
Last night I thought he stood beside my bed,
And said, ' Wake up! You were dreaming. I am here.'

3

Take any grief—the maggot at the nerve,
The words that bore the skull like waterdrops,
The castaway's upon the foam-racked island,
The lurching figures of a mind's eclipse—
I have felt each and all as love decayed.

Yet every pang revives a fainting love.
They are love's children too; I live again
In them; my breast yearns to their innocent cruelty.
If only tears can float a stranded heart,
If only sighs can move it, I will grieve.

The pleasured nerve, the small-talk in the night,
The voyaging when isles were daisy-chains,
The dance of shared routine—if I could reach them
Again through this sick labyrinth of grief,
I would rejoice in it, to reach them so.

Alas, hull-down upon hope's ashen verge
Hastens the vessel that our joined hands launched,
Stretching my heart-strings out beyond endurance.
Ah, will they never snap? Then I must climb
The signal hill, and wave, and *mean* goodbye.

4

Oh lenient be the airs for him
That from the south-west blow,
And may this lamb forgiving lie
Forgotten in the snow!

Oh cleaving be the airs that fall,
Bitter their memoried blows
Between him and his fancy one,
Till he my numb grief knows!

Louis MacNeice

THE DRUNKARD

His last train home is Purgatory in reverse,
A spiral back into time and down towards Hell
Clutching a quizzical strap where wraiths of faces
Contract, expand, revolve, impinge; disperse
On a sickly wind which drives all wraiths pell-mell
Through tunnels towards their appointed, separate places.

And he is separate too, who had but now ascended
Into the panarchy of created things
Wearing his halo cocked, full of good will
That need not be implemented; time stood still
As the false coin rang and the four walls had wings
And instantly the Natural Man was mended.

Instantly and it would be permanently
God was uttered in words and gulped in gin,
The barmaid was a Madonna, the adoration
Of the coalman's breath was myrrh, the world was We
And pissing under the stars an act of creation
While the low hills lay purring round the inn.

Such was the absolute moment, to be displaced
By moments; the clock takes over—times to descend
Again into time, whose brief is to depress
The man who looks and finds Man human and not his friend
And whose tongue feels around and around but cannot taste
That hour-gone sacrament of drunkenness.

Ivan Bunin

TANYA

Translated from the Russian by Richard Hare

SHE WAS working as a housemaid in the house of his relation Madame Kazakov, who owned a small estate. She was just seventeen years old, very small, which was especially noticeable when she walked barefoot, her skirt swaying gently from side to side and her little breasts moving under her blouse, or when she stood in winter in her felt boots; her simple little face could only be called attractive, and her grey peasant eyes had no beauty other than that of youth. In those far-off days he used to embark on every kind of senseless adventure, he led a roving life, had many chance love affairs—and his relationship with her started as a casual affair of this kind . . .

She soon reconciled herself to that surprising stroke of fate which befell her one autumn evening; for a few days she wept, but every day she became more and more convinced that what had happened was no misfortune, but a happiness, that he was becoming every day dearer to her; in moments of intimacy, which soon began to recur quite often, she already called him Petrushka and spoke of that night as if it were something sacred belonging to their past.

At first he both believed and doubted;

'Is it really true you weren't just pretending to sleep that night?'

She only opened her eyes more widely;

'But didn't you realize that I was sleeping, don't you know how soundly children and young girls sleep?'

'If I had known you really were asleep, I should never have touched you.'

'Well, and I simply didn't feel anything almost up to the last moment! But how did it enter your head to come to me? When you arrived you hardly looked at me, only in the evening you asked, so she's new here, is she called Tanya? and then you looked away without paying any more attention to me. So you were only pretending?'

He answered that of course he was pretending, but he did not speak the truth; for him also it had all happened quite unexpectedly. He had spent the early autumn in the Crimea and on his way back to Moscow had stopped to visit Kazakova, spending a fortnight in the soothing simplicity of her country life; when the dim November days began he got ready to leave. Taking leave of the countryside on that day, he rode about from morning till night with a gun over his shoulder and accompanied by a sporting dog, guiding his horse over empty fields and through treeless woods; he found no game and returned to the house tired and hungry, ate for supper a panful of beef cutlets with sour cream, emptied a small decanter of vodka and some glasses of tea, while Kazakova, as always, went on talking about her late husband and her two sons who were in government service at Orla. By ten o'clock it was quite dark in the house; only a candle was burning in the study next to the drawing-room, where he was put up when he stayed in the house. When he entered the study, she was kneeling on his bed, a converted sofa, waving a flaring candle close to the plank wall. Seeing him, she dropped the candle on the night table, and jumping down, ran from the room.

'What is it?' he asked in amazement. 'Wait a moment, what on earth were you doing?'

'I was burning a bug,' she answered in a hurried whisper. 'I was arranging your bed, when I looked up and saw a bug on the wall . . .'

And she ran off laughing.

He watched her go, and without undressing, only removing his long boots, he lay down on the quilted cover on the sofa, intending to smoke and turn things over in his mind—he was unaccustomed to going to bed at ten o'clock—but he fell asleep at once. He woke up for a moment, disturbed in a dream by the guttering candle-flame, blew it out and fell asleep again. The next time he opened his eyes, the brilliant light of the autumn moon was pouring in through the two windows facing the courtyard and from the wide window on to the garden; the night had an empty and lonely beauty. He found his slippers near the sofa and went out into the passage leading to the back door—they had forgotten to leave for him what was necessary at night. But the next door seemed to be bolted from the other side, so he went round to the front hall through the mysteriously illuminated house. From there the main passage led into a large wooden ante-room. In the passage opposite a tall window over an old locker, stood a partition, behind which was a room without windows, where the maids always slept. The door through the partition was open, but it was dark inside. He lit a match and caught sight of her asleep. She was lying on her back on a wooden bed, in a blouse and cotton skirt—her little breasts showed their roundness through the blouse, her legs were bare to the knees, her right arm, pressed against the wall, and her face on the pillow looked still as death. . . . The match went out. He stood there—and gently approached the bed . . .

Going back through the dark ante-room into the hall he thought feverishly;

'How strange, how unexpected! Could she really have been asleep?'

He stood in the porch and went outside. . . . It was an extraordinary night. The broad open courtyard was brilliantly lit up by the high moon. On the opposite side stood a shed piled up with old straw—a cattle-shed, the coach-house and stables. And everything around had its own uncanny night existence, detached from human beings, shining for no reason; it was still more uncanny to him because it seemed to be the first time he saw this world of a summer's night. . . .

He sat down near the coach-house on the footboard of a carriage streaked with dry mud. The warm air smelt like an autumn garden, the night was wonderful, serene, benevolent, and somehow harmonized surprisingly with those feelings which he had borne away from that unexpected union with a half-childish girl. . . .

She wept softly when she came to herself and began to understand what had happened, what she had hardly realized before. Her whole body had yielded to him without any life of its own. First he had urged her in a whisper, 'Don't be frightened, listen . . .'

She heard nothing or pretended not to hear. He quietly kissed her warm cheek—she did not respond to the kiss, and he thought that she silently consented to whatever might ensue. He moved her legs apart in their tender warmth—she only sighed in her sleep, slightly stretched herself and put one hand behind her head . . .

'But if it was not pretence?' he thought, getting up from the footboard and looking excitedly around him.

When she wept, sweetly and pathetically, he felt not only animal gratitude for that unexpected happiness which she had unconsciously given him, but a kind of enthusiasm and love, and he began to kiss her neck, her breast, inhaling that intoxicating scent of something rural and virginal. And she, through her tears, suddenly gave a spontaneous feminine response—strongly, and it seemed gratefully, embracing him and pressing his head to her breast. In her half-wakeful state she did not know who he was—but no matter—he was the man with whom at some time she was bound to be linked in the most mysterious and sacred intimacy. That mutual link had been forged, nothing in the world could break it, he carried it within him for ever, and now this

35

extraordinary night received him into its inscrutable moonlit kingdom together with that bond . . .

How could he, when he left, remember her only casually, or forget her sweet affectionate little voice, her joyous or melancholy but always loving and submissive eyes, how could he ever love others who would mean more to him than her!

The following day she served at table without raising her eyes. Kazakova asked;

'What is the matter with you, Tanya?'

She answered respectfully;

'I have some trouble, Madam . . .'

Kazakova said to him when she went out;

'Well, of course, she's an orphan, without a mother, her father is a wandering beggar . . .'

Towards evening when she was arranging the samovar in the hall, he passed by and said to her;

'You won't believe it, but I've loved you for a long time. Stop weeping and tormenting yourself, you won't gain anything by that . . .'

She answered, dropping red hot charcoal into the samovar;

'If you really loved me, how much easier it would all be . . .'

Then she used sometimes to glance up at him as if she were timidly enquiring; is it true?

One evening when she had gone to prepare his bed, he came up behind her and embraced her round the shoulder. She cast a frightened glance at him, and whispered, blushing all over;

'Go away, for God's sake. The old woman will come in at any moment . . .'

'What old woman?'

'The old housemaid, you know her!'

'I'll come to you tonight . . .'

She was burning—the old woman terrified her;

'Oh, what are you saying. I shall go mad with fright!'

'Well, there's no need, don't be afraid, I won't come,' he said hurriedly.

She was again working as before, quickly and efficiently, constantly darted backwards and forwards between the courtyard and the kitchen, as she used to, and sometimes, seizing a favourable moment, secretly cast at him looks of embarrassed joy. And one day at dawn, while he was sleeping, they sent her into the town to do some shopping. At lunch Kazakova said to him;

'What shall I do, I sent the agent with a workman to the windmill,

I've no one to send to the station for Tanya. Perhaps you wouldn't mind going? '

Restraining his joy, he answered with pretended indifference;
' Of course, I'll gladly go.'

The old housemaid, who was serving at table, frowned;
' Why, Madam, do you want to bring the girl to lasting shame? What will they say about her in the village after that? '

' Well, go there yourself,' said Kazakova. ' Do you expect the girl to walk from the station ? '

About four o'clock he went off in a gig drawn by a tall old black mare, pressing her on to avoid being late for the train, sliding over the greasy road which had frozen and thawed again—the last few days had been damp and misty, and that day the fog was particularly dense; when he was driving through the village it seemed that night had fallen and hazy red lights were visible in the huts, wild patches in the enveloping mist. Further on, in the fields, it grew quite dark and one could not see through the fog at all. A cold wind blew in his face, but it did not disperse the fog—on the contrary, it compressed still more densely those cold dark-grey clouds, filling them with damp fumes, and it looked as if nothing lay beyond that impenetrable mist—only the end of the world and of everything alive. His cap, his coat, eyelashes and moustache were all covered with tiny beads of moisture. The black mare lurched along and the carriage, jolting over the slippery ruts, shook his bones. He leaned over and started to smoke—the sweet aromatic warm human smoke of the cigarette mingled with the primeval smell of fog, late autumn and damp bare fields. And everything around grew darker and gloomier—he could hardly see the dim outline of the horse's long neck and pricked-up ears. And he felt increasingly near to the horse—to the only live being in that wilderness, in that deadly enmity of everything around to right and left, behind and in front, of all that lay unknown, ominously hidden in the ever thicker and blacker waves of those smoky depths . . .

When he reached the village near the station, he rejoiced at the signs of human habitation, the pathetic little lights in the squalid windows, their affectionate cosiness—and the station itself seemed to him like another world, lively, cheerful and urban. And he had hardly managed to tie up the horse before the train came thundering into the station; its windows were all lit up and it exuded an acrid smell of burning coal. He ran on to the platform feeling as if he were going to meet a newly-married wife, and immediately caught sight of her dragging two large shopping bags out of a carriage facing the station-master's office. The station was dirty and reeked from the oil of the kerosene lamps which lit it dimly; she was dressed in her town clothes, her eyes were bright with youthful excitement about the unaccustomed journey, and the station-master made some polite remark to her. Suddenly her eyes met his and she stopped in confusion. What could it mean, why was he here?

' Tanya,' he said hurriedly; ' Good day, I've come to fetch you. There was no one else to send . . . '

Had she ever known in her life such a happy evening? . . . He came to meet me himself, and I was all dressed up and much prettier than he had ever imagined, having only seen me in the same old skirt, in a plain cotton blouse—but I looked as if I had just come out of a dressmaker's shop in that white silk scarf and new brown woollen dress under a little cloth jacket, white cotton stockings and new half-boots with brass buckles. . . . With inward trembling she spoke to him in the tone of a newly-arrived visitor, and lifting up the hem of her skirt, she followed him with dainty lady-like steps, as if on the point of exclaiming indulgently; ' Oh, my God, how slippery, how the peasants have trampled the mud!' Her heart sinking with delighted fear, she raised her dress high over her white calico petticoat, in order to sit on the petticoat and not on the dress, got into the carriage and sat down beside him as if she were his equal, awkwardly arranging the bags at her feet.

He silently flicked at the horse and they started off into the icy darkness and fog, passing the low lights of the huts, jolting over the holes in that deplorable country road, and she, terrified of his silence, did not dare to utter a word; had something made him angry with her? He understood what she felt and purposely remained silent. And suddenly, leaving the village behind and plunging into complete darkness, he brought the horse to a walking pace, gathered the reins together in his left hand and with his right pressed her shoulder in its little jacket covered with beads of moisture, laughing and muttering;

' Tanya, Tanechka . . . '

And she pressed herself to him, her silk scarf and tender flushed face touching his cheek, her eyelashes glistening with hot tears. He found her lips, also wet with joyful tears, stopped the horse, and kissed her for a long time. Then like a blind man, without seeing a thing in the dark fog, he got out of the carriage, and threw his coat on the ground, turning the sleeves inwards. Understanding at once, she immediately jumped down to join him, and with deft hands lifting up all her precious clothes, her new dress and petticoat, she lay down quivering on the coat, and surrendered to him for ever not only her body, which was entirely his, but also her whole soul.

He again postponed his journey. She knew this was on account of her, she saw how affectionate he was with her, talking to her like an intimate secret friend in the house; and she was no longer frightened and trembling when he approached her, as she had been at first. He grew quieter and simpler when they met—she quickly adapted herself to him. She had completely changed, with that rapidity of which only youth is capable, and showed a calm carefree happiness, gaily called him Petrushka, sometimes even pretended that he kissed her more than she wanted; ' My God, there's no getting away from you! The moment he sees me alone, here he comes! '—and that gave her a special kind of pleasure; it means he must love me, he is entirely mine, if I can talk to him like that! Yet another joy for her was to express to him her jealousy, her right to possess him;

' Thank God there is no work on the threshing-floor, because if there were girls there, I should have had to show you the way to them! ' she said.

And she added, feeling suddenly shy, with a touching attempt to smile;

' Is it too little for you to have only me? '

Winter set in early. After the fogs came an icy north wind, hardening the uneven muddy roads, turning the earth to stone and withering the last grass in the garden and courtyard. Leaden clouds covered the sky, the bare garden rustled disconsolately, abruptly, as if it were slinking away, at night the white half-moon dived in and out of banks of cloud. The park and the village looked terribly poor, petty and vulgar. Next came a fall of snow, whitening the cold dirt like powdered sugar, and the park and fields beyond it became greyish-white and spacious. They finished the last work out of doors—spread the potatoes in the cellar for the winter, sorting them out and throwing away the rotten ones. He walked about the countryside wearing his short fox fur-coat and a fur cap pushed over his forehead. The north wind whistled through his moustache and made his cheeks tingle. Under a gloomy overcast sky the greyish white sloping fields across the river seemed very near. In the village huge scales lay on the ground near piles of potatoes. Sitting on these scales, women and girls were working, huddled in hempen shawls with ragged jackets and worn-out boots, their faces and hands blue with cold—he thought with horror; surely under their skirts they have nothing but naked legs!

When he came home, she was standing in the hall, wiping the boiling samovar with a cloth before she carried it to the table, and immediately she exclaimed in a whisper;

' So you've been walking through the village, girls are sorting out potatoes there. . . . Very well, you'd better go on walking till you can find someone better! '

And, restraining her tears, she ran away into the pantry.

Towards evening the snow piled up more and more thickly, and passing him in the drawing-room she glanced at him with an outburst of childish gaiety, and whispered teasingly;

'Well, are you still walking a lot? What will happen—dogs are running about all over the yard——'

'My God,' he thought, 'how shall I ever pluck up courage to tell her that I'm going away so soon.'

And he felt an absolute longing to be back in Moscow as quickly as possible. Frost, snowstorms in the Iversky Square, steaming steak rolled up in cabbage leaves, tinkling sleigh-bells, on the boulevard the high electric light from the lamps seen through the snow blizzard. . . . In the Great Theatre the chandeliers are glittering to the strains of harmonious music, and he, throwing his snowy fur-coat into the arms of an attendant, wiping the wet snow from his moustache, walks cheerfully as usual over the red carpet through the warm crowded stalls, through the hum of conversation, the smell of food and cigarettes, among the fussy attendants and the all-embracing waves of music from the orchestra, rise up caressingly languid, stormy or rollicking . . .

During the whole of supper he could not raise his eyes to her carefree serene face, as she ran backwards and forwards.

Late in the evening he put on his long boots and an old raccoon coat which had belonged to the late Kazakov, pushed his cap forward and went through the back door into the blizzard, sniffing the air. But a whole snowdrift had already formed under the roof of the porch, he slipped into it and his sleeves were covered with snow, and further on was a white hell of deep drifts; constantly sinking in, he got round the house with difficulty, reached the front porch, and stamping his feet and shaking himself entered the dark ante-room, and then passed into the warm passage where a candle was burning on the locker. She jumped out bare-footed from behind the partition, dressed in the same cotton skirt, throwing up her arms;

'My God, where have you sprung from!'

He threw his coat and cap on the locker, sprinkling it with snow, and in a mad transport of tenderness seized her hands. She tore herself away in excitement, seized a brush and began to wipe the snow from his boots and pull them off;

'My God, they're full of snow too! You'll catch your death of cold!'

Through his sleep that night he occasionally heard how the wind howled monotonously round the house, then rose to a climax, beating snow against the window panes, shaking them—and died down again, passing further away, moaning drowsily. . . . The night seemed endless

and sweet—in the warmth of the bed, of the old house, alone in the
white depths of the mounting sea of snow . . .

In the morning it seemed that the wind was bursting open the window-
panes—he opened his eyes—no, it was already light, and with a dazzling
whiteness from the snow piled up over the window-sills, and casting
white reflections on the ceiling. A wind was still blowing, but it was
quieter, more like day-time. From the corner of the sofa one could
see two windows opposite with double frames blackened with age, the
third window, on the left, was the whitest and brightest of the lot. The
white reflection lay on the ceiling, but in the corner the door of the
stove quivered and hummed while the draught fanned the flames inside
—how pleasant it was—he had been asleep and heard nothing, but Tanya,
the faithful loving Tanechka, had pulled up the blinds, gone quietly in
her boots, chilly from snow, had knelt down and lit the stove. And he
had hardly gathered his wits together when she came in again, carrying a
tray with tea, this time without a scarf. Putting down the tray on the
small table near the pillow, with a scarcely perceptible smile she looked
into his clear eyes still dazed by sleep;

' How did you manage to sleep so late? '

' But what time is it? ' She looked at the clock on the table and did
not answer at once—she still found it difficult to read the time;

' Ten . . . ten minutes to nine . . . '

With a glance at the door he pulled her towards him by the skirt.
She turned away, removing his hand.

' You really can't, everyone is awake . . . '

' Just for one minute! '

' The old woman may come in . . . '

' No one will come in—just for a minute! '

' Oh, I'm punished with you! '

Quickly drawing her feet in woollen stockings out of their boots,
she lay down, looking round at the door. . . . Oh, that peasant smell of
her head, her breath, the apple coolness of her cheek! He whispered
angrily;

' Again you kiss with compressed lips! When shall I be able to teach
you? '

' I'm not a lady. . . . Wait a moment, I'll lie lower down. . . . Be
quick, I'm frightened to death.'

And they stared into each other's eyes—fixedly, blankly, expectantly.

' Petrushka . . . '

' Be silent. Why do you always speak at such a moment! '

' But when can I speak to you except at such moments! I won't
compress my lips any more . . . do you swear to me that you have
no one in Moscow . . . '

' Don't squeeze my neck so hard . . . '

' No one else will ever love you as I do. And since you've fallen in love with me, I feel as if I loved myself. But if you throw me over . . . '

Going with a flushed face through the porch at the back door, she sat down for a moment, then dashed through the white drifts leading to the front porch, sinking in above her knees.

The samovar was burning in the hall. The old housemaid, sitting on the locker under a high window, was sipping tea from a saucer, and without putting it down she squinted at Tanya;

' Where have you come from? All plunged in snow.'

' I was giving tea to Pyotr Nikolaich.'

' And what did you give him in the servants' room? We know what your tea is! '

' Whatever you know, may it do you good. Has the mistress got up yet? '

' I should think so! Earlier than you.'

' Well, you're always angry.'

And, sighing happily, she went outside with her cup, singing in an undertone;

> ' So I go into the garden,
> The green garden,
> To walk through the green garden,
> And meet my dear one there . . . '

During the day, sitting in the study over a book, listening to the same gale blowing round the house, sometimes calming down, sometimes rising to a fury, drowning everything more and more under masses of milk-white snow—he thought; as soon as the storm is over, I must leave.

In the evening he found an opportunity to tell her to come to him late that night when everyone was fast asleep—to stay the whole night till morning. She shook her head, reflected for a moment and said: ' Very well.' It was terrifying, but all the more wonderful.

He felt in much the same way but he was also torn by pity for her —she had no idea it would be their last night! At night he kept on falling asleep and waking up from excitement; would she really come? It was pitch dark, the wind shook the window panes and sometimes howled through the chimney. . . . Suddenly he woke up in a fright, he heard nothing—it was impossible to hear her in that criminal caution with which she groped through the darkness of the house—he heard nothing, yet he felt that she was already standing there, invisible, near the sofa. He stretched out his hand. She silently dived under the blanket to join him. He heard how her heart was beating, felt her chilled bare

42

feet and whispered the very warmest words he could find and express.

Thus they lay for a long time, breast clasped to breast, and kissing so strongly that their teeth were sore. She remembered he had told her not to close her lips, and in her efforts to please him she opened her mouth like a jackdaw.

' Didn't you sleep at all? '

She answered in a happy whisper;

' Not for a second. I was waiting all the time . . . '

He fumbled for the matches on the table and lit the candle. She uttered a frightened sound;

' Petrushka, what are you doing? If the old woman wakes up and sees the light . . . '

' Let her go to the devil,' he said, looking at her little flushed face. ' I want to see you . . . '

Embracing her, he did not take his eyes from her. She whispered;

' I'm afraid—why do you look at me so? '

' Because there's nothing better than you in the world. That little head with the little pigtail round it, like the young Venus . . . '

Her eyes sparkled with laughter and happiness;

' What is that Venus? '

' It's you . . . and that little blouse . . . '

' But you'll buy me some fine muslin. . . . It's true you really love me very much! '

' No, I don't love you at all! And again you smell rather like a quail or dried hemp . . . '

' Why do you like that? You were telling me I always spoke at these moments . . . but now you speak yourself . . . '

She began to press him to her still more strongly, wanted to say something more, but could not . . .

Afterwards he put out the candle and lay for a long time in silence, smoking and thinking; but all the same I ought to tell her; it's awful, but I must! And he began in a scarcely audible whisper;

' Tanechka . . . '

' What is it? ' she asked in an equally mysterious whisper.

' You know I shall have to go away.'

She raised herself;

' When? '

' Well, soon . . . very soon . . . I have business which can't be put off . . . '

She fell back on the pillow.

' My God! '

That business of his somewhere over there in a place called Moscow filled her with a kind of awe. But all the same how could she be separated

43

from him on account of those affairs? She said nothing, quickly but helplessly seeking in her mind a way out from this insoluble horror. There was no way out. She wanted to exclaim; ' Take me with you! ' But she did not dare—could it be possible?

' I can't live here forever . . . '

She listened and agreed; ' yes, yes ' . . .

' I can't take you away with me . . . '

She burst out in despair;

' Why? '

He thought quickly; ' Yes, why? why not? '—and hurriedly answered; ' I have no home, Tanya, all the time I travel from one place to another. . . . In Moscow I live in an hotel. . . . And never in my life will I marry anyone . . . '

' Why? '

' Because I was born like that.'

' So you will never marry anyone? '

' No one, never! I give you my word of honour—I really have important business which I can't put off. At Christmas I'll come back here again! '

Her head fell on his shoulder, she lay there shedding hot tears, and whispered;

' Well, I must go . . . it will soon be light.'

She got up and stood in the darkness, crossing him;

' May the Heavenly Empress preserve you, may the Mother of God preserve you! '

She hurried back to her partition, sat down on the bed, pressing her hands to her breasts, and licking the tears from her lips, she began to whisper through the noise of the storm;

' Father God, Heavenly Empress! God grant that the storm will go on for two days longer! '

Two days later he went away—the whirlwind outside was only starting to calm down, but he could not prolong the hidden torment they both felt and he resisted Kazakova's entreaties that he should stay at least till the next day.

The house and the whole place grew empty and dead. It was quite impossible to imagine Moscow and how he lived there, what he was doing.

He did not come at Christmas—what days those were! What a torture of unresolved expectancy, what pathetic efforts to deceive herself when there was obviously no point in expecting him any longer—so the time passed from morning till evening! During the whole Christmas festival she walked about in her best clothes—the same dress and half-boots which she was wearing when he met her that autumn on the station platform, on that unforgettable evening.

When Epiphany came, for some reason she greedily seized on the belief that at any moment peasant sleighs would appear over the hill, that he had hired them at the station, having arrived without warning that he would want horses sent; all day long she lay on the locker in the passage, looking out into the courtyard with an aching pain in her eyes. The house was empty—Kazakova had gone to visit some neighbours, the old housemaid was eating in the servants' hall, and she went on sitting there after dinner, enjoying an exchange of scandal with the cook. Tanya did not even get up for a meal, she said her stomach ached . . .

But night was falling. She looked again into the empty shining courtyard, and got up, saying firmly to herself; this is the end of it all, I need no one any more, I don't want to wait for anything!—and she walked deliberately, all dressed up, through the hall, through the drawing-room, lit through the windows by the yellow winter sunset, and sang in a loud carefree voice—relieved that a lifetime had come to an end;

> ' So I go into the garden,
> The green garden,
> To walk through the green garden,
> And meet my dear one there! '

And just as she was singing those last words she came into the study, saw his empty sofa, the empty arm-chair alongside the writing table, where he once sat with a book in his hands, and she sank into that chair with her head on the table, weeping and crying at the top of her voice: ' Heavenly Empress, let me die! '

He came in February—when she had already buried her last hopes of seeing him even once again in life.

And it seemed that everything became as it had been before. He was shocked when he saw her—she had grown so thin and pale, her eyes were so furtive and sad. She too was shocked in the first moments; he seemed to her different, older, a strange person, almost unpleasant—his moustache seemed larger, his voice coarser, his laugh and the remarks he made in the hall, while he was taking off his coat, were unnecessarily loud and artificial; she found it embarrassing to look into his eyes. . . .

45

But they both tried to conceal all this from each other and soon it seemed that everything came back as before.

Then again the terrible time approached—the time for him to leave. He swore to her on the ikon that he would come at Whitsuntide and stay for the whole summer. She believed him, but she thought; 'And what will happen in summer? Will it be the same as now?' That meant little enough to her now—it must either be entirely, genuinely as it was before, not a mere repetition, or it must be a continuous life with him without separations, without renewed torments, without the shame of all those disappointed hopes. But she tried to chase this thought from her mind, tried to imagine all that summer happiness, when they would have so much freedom everywhere—night and day, in the garden, the fields, in the barn, and he would be close to her for a long, long time . . .

On the eve of his next departure the night was bright and showery, like a forecast of spring. The garden rustled behind the house, and borne by the wind from the same direction came the intermittent, angry but helpless barking of dogs over a pit in the pinewood; inside the pit was a vixen which had been caught in a trap and brought to the house by Kazakova's gamekeeper.

He was lying on the sofa on his back with closed eyes. She lay on her side, next to him, with one hand clasped under her thoughtful little head. Both were silent. At last she whispered:

'Petrushka, are you asleep?'

He opened his eyes, looked round in the half-darkness of the room, lit with a golden light from a window on the left side;

'No. What is it?'

'Surely you don't love me any more, you ruined me for nothing,' she said quietly.

'What do you mean, for nothing? Don't talk nonsense.'

'You sinned in doing that. Where can I go now?'

'But why should you go anywhere?'

'Once again you go away to your Moscow, and what can I do here alone?'

'But just the same as you did before. And later on—surely I promised you definitely; I'll come here for the whole summer.'

'Yes, maybe you will come. . . . But you used not to say such words to me before; "but why should you go anywhere?" You truly loved me then, you told me you had never seen anyone sweeter than me. Yes, was I really like that?'

'No, she is not any longer,' he thought, 'she has altered terribly. Even her body has withered, all the small bones stick out . . .'

46

'My little hour has passed,' she said. 'I used to run to you before, scared to death and rejoicing, thank God, the old woman has gone to sleep. But now I'm not even frightened of her . . . '

He shrugged his shoulders;

'I don't understand you. Give me the cigarettes from the table . . . '

She handed them to him. He lit one.

'I don't know what's the matter with you. You're simply un-well . . . '

'Surely that's why I'm no longer dear to you. And what do you think has made me ill?'

'You don't understand me. I mean you are spiritually unwell—please think for a moment, what has happened, what has made you imagine that I no longer love you? And why should you go on repeating that word, before, before . . . ?'

She made no answer. The dawn glimmered through the window, the garden rustled, from beyond rose intermittently the angry, desperate plaintive yelping of dogs. . . . She slid quietly from the sofa, and pressing her sleeve to her eyes with her head bowed, she walked softly in her woollen stockings towards the door. He called after her in a low but firm voice;

'Tanya.'

She turned round and answered almost inaudibly;

'What do you want?'

'Come here to me.'

'What for?'

'I tell you, come here.'

She came obediently, bending her head to prevent him from seeing that her face was covered with tears.

'Well, what do you want?'

'Sit down and don't cry. Kiss me—well?'

He sat down, she sat beside him and embraced him, weeping quietly. 'My God, what should I do!' he thought in despair. 'Again those hot childish tears on the flushed childish face. . . . She doesn't even suspect the whole strength of my feeling for her! But what can I do? Take her away with me? Where? To what kind of life? And what would be the result? To bind oneself, ruin oneself for ever?' And he hurriedly began to whisper to her, feeling how his own tears were tickling his nose and lips;

'Tanechka, my joy, don't cry, listen; I'll come in spring for the whole summer, and then we will really walk together " in the green garden " —I heard you singing that little song and I'll never forget it—we will drive in the carriage through the woods—do you remember how we came in the carriage from the station?'

'No one will let me go with you!' she whispered bitterly, letting her head fall on his breast. 'And you will never drive with me any more . . .'

But he already detected in her voice a note of timid joy and hope.

'I will come and be with you, indeed I will, Tanechka! And you must always call me by my first name. And don't you dare to weep . . .'

He lifted her up by the legs in her woollen stockings and laid her light body over his knees;

'Now say: "Petrushka, I love you very much."'

She numbly repeated, choking from sobs;

'I love you very much . . .'

That was in February of the terrible year, 1917. He was staying there in the country for the last time in his life.

George Seferis

THE THRUSH

Translated from the Greek by Rex Warner

I

The House Near The Sea

THE HOUSES that I had they took from me. It happened
the times were out of joint. Wars, waste and exiles.
Sometimes the hunter gets the birds of passage
sometimes he does not get them. There was in my time
good hunting. Bursts of fire took a heavy toll.
The others turn round and round or go mad in the shelters.

Do not speak to me of the nightingale, do not speak of the lark
do not speak of the little wagtail
who with his tail writes figures on the light.
I do not know a great deal about houses:
I know how houses are, and that is all.
They are new at first, new like babies
who play in gardens with the tassels of the sun,
they do their embroideries with coloured shutters
and doors brilliantly shining on the screen of the day.
When the architect has finished, then they change,
they wrinkle up, they smile, or again grow obstinate
with those who stayed behind and with those who left,
with others who would return there if they could,
or who have become lost now that this has happened,—
the world become a limitless inn for strangers.

I do not know a great deal about houses.
I remember their joy and their sorrow
sometimes, when I stand still.
                                        And also
at times, near the sea, in rooms stripped naked,
with a single iron bedstead and nothing that is mine,

D   49

looking at the evening spider I call to mind
how such a one is getting ready to come, how they clothe him
in clothes of white and black and with coloured jewels,
and around him is the slow speech of respected ladies,
with their grey hair and their dark lace,
how he gets ready to come to say goodbye to me.
Or a woman deep-girdled, with glancing eyes,
returning home from harbours of the south,
Smyrna, Rhodes, Syracuse, Alexandria,
from cities closed like shutters closed in the heat,
with perfume of golden fruit, and aromatic herbs,
how she is climbing the stairs without paying attention
to those who have gone to sleep underneath the stairs.

You find houses get obstinate easily, when you strip them naked.

II

The Lusty Elpenor

I saw him yesterday stop by the door,
down from my window. It was round about
seven o'clock and there was a woman with him.
He had the look of Elpenor just before
he fell and broke; and yet he was not drunk.
He was speaking very quickly, and the woman
looked in an absent way towards the gramophones.
She stopped him occasionally to say a word or two
and then she would look away impatiently
to where they were frying fish. Like a cat looks.
He whispered with a fag-end in his lips:

' Listen again to this. I have seen by moonlight
sometimes the statues leaning over like reeds
in the middle of living fruit,—the statues,
and the flame becomes a dewy oleander,
the flame that burns the man, I mean to say.'

' A trick of the light . . . the effect of the night shadows '

' The night perhaps: which opened, a blue pomegranate,
dark breasts, filling you full of stars,
cutting down time.
                              But all the same the statues

50

sometimes do bend, and they deal out desire
into two parts, like a peach shared, and the flame
becomes a kiss on the limbs, a sobbing of breath
and then a cool leaf the wind carries away.
They bend, they become light with a human weight.
You cannot forget it.'
                                    ' The statues are in the museum.'

' No it is you they hunt. Why can't you see?
I mean the statues with their broken limbs
and faces from another time you have never
seen, and yet you know them.
                                        It is like
at the end of your youth you happen to be in love
with a woman who has kept her beauty. Always,
holding her naked body in the noon,
you fear the memory that surges up
to your embrace, you fear the kiss betraying you
to other beds which now are in time past,
and yet, for all that, there are ghosts might stalk there
easily, so easily, and bring to life
images to the mirror, bodies that were once,
and all the lust they had then.
                                        It is like
coming back from a foreign land you chance to open
an old chest that for long has been locked up;
and there you find bits and pieces of the dresses
you wore in lovely times, in lighted dances
of many colours, mirrored, which all fade,
and remains only the perfume of the absence
of a young face.
                        Oh it is true; the fragments
are not the statues. You are yourself the remains.
    They haunt you with their strange virginity
at home or office, at the big receptions
for honoured people, in your unconfessed
terror of sleep. They speak of what you wish
had never happened, or could happen years
after your death. Difficult, because——'
                                    ' The statues are in the museum.
Good night.'
' —because the statues are no more fragments.
We are. The statues lightly bend. . . . Good night.'

At this they separated and he took
the upper road that leads towards the Bear.
And she went forward to the lighted beach
where the wave is drowned in the roar of the radio:

The Radio

' Sails in the breath of the wind
that was all that the mind
kept of the day, silence and scent of the pine.
Easily they will cover the wound that is mine
the wound that they made when they left me behind
the sailor, the wagtail, the bullhead, the flycatcher too.
O woman insensitive, you,
hear of the death of the wind.

The golden barrel is done
and a rag is what was the sun,
a rag on the neck of a woman in middle age
who coughs and who never stops coughing. What can assuage
her grief for the summer that journeyed and left her behind,
for the gold on the shoulders and gold in the pit of the thighs?
O woman deprived of your eyes,
hear me, the singer is blind.

Night falls. Shut the house fast
Make flutes of the reeds of the past.
Open the window no more, however much they
knock at the pane. They shout but have nothing to say.
Bring cyclamen, bring needles of pine and grasses,
lilies out of the sand and anemones out of the sea.
O woman, mindless, hear me,
The water's funeral passes.

Athens. The situation rapidly
deteriorates. The public are alarmed.
The Minister declared " No time is left ". . . .
Bring cyclamen and bring the pine needles. . . .
and lilies from the sand . . . and pine needles
O woman . . . . There is an immense disparity.
The war—'
       Ares, dealer in souls—

III

The Wreck Of ' The Thrush '

' This wood which used to bring refreshment to my brow
in times when mid-day sun put fire into the veins,
in foreign hands will blossom. Take it. I give it you.
Look, the wood is of a lemon tree.'
          I heard the voice
when, staring into the sea, I tried to distinguish
a ship which many years ago they had sunk there.
The ship's name was ' The Thrush ', a small wreck, and the masts,
broken, groped to the bottom oblique, like tentacles,
or memory of dreams, indicating the hull,
an indistinguishable mouth of some sea-creature, dead,
quenched in the water. There was total calm around.

And little by little other voices in their turn
followed in whisperings; they were thin and thirsty
and came from the other side of the sun, the dark side;
you would say they sought to drink blood, just a drop of it.
Familiar voices but I could not recognise them.
And then there came that old man's voice, this one I felt
drop to the heart of the day
calm, changeless, still:
' If you sentence me to drink the poison, I thank you.
Your law shall be made my law. And where should I go
running about in foreign lands, a rolling stone?
I choose death rather.
Which of us goes to the better fate God knows.'
Lands of sun, where you cannot face the sun!
Lands of man, where you cannot face the man!

The Light

As the years pass
so increase in number the judges who condemn you,
as the years pass and you speak with fewer voices
you look with other eyes upon the sun.
You know that those who remained were cheating you,
flesh's delirium, the lovely dance
that ends in nakedness.
As when, at night, turning into an empty highway

you suddenly see an animal's shining eyes
which have already gone, so you feel your own eyes:
you stare at the sun: and then you are lost in the dark.
The doric chiton
your fingers touched and it bent like the mountains
is a marble image in light, but its head is in darkness.
And those who left the palaestra to take their bows
and shot the marathon runner full of the will to win;
and he saw the laps of the track sailing in blood
the world grow empty like the waning moon,
victorious gardens withering away;
you see them in the sun, behind the sun.
And the boys who were doing diving from the bow-sprits
go down like spindles, spinning round and round,
bare bodies plunging into the black light,
with a coin between the teeth, still swimming on,
as the sun picks out with golden needlework
sails, wet wood and colours of the deep sea;
even now they go down obliquely
down to the stones of the deep,
white shining jars.

Black angel light,
laughter of waves on high ways of the sea,
laughter between the tears,
the old man in supplication looks on you
as he makes his way over invisible folds,
light mirrored in that blood
from which sprang Eteokles and Polynikes.
Black angel day;
the brackish taste of woman that poisons the captive
springs from the wave, fresh sprig, with sea drops on it;
O sing, little Antigone, sing, O sing . . .
I do not speak of the past, I speak of love;
crown your hair with thorns of the sun, dark girl.
The heart of the Scorpion has set,
the Tyrant inside man has gone,
and all the daughters of the deep,
Nereids, Graiae
run to the dazzle of the springs of light.
He who has never loved shall love in the light.
                              And you find yourself
in a great house with many windows open

running from room to room, not knowing where first to look out.
Because the pines will go, and the mirrored mountains
and the chirping of birds.
The sea will empty, shattered glass, from North and South.
Your eyes will be emptied of the light of the day
as suddenly, of one accord, all the cicadas cease.

Odysseus Elytis

TWO POEMS

Translated from the Greek by Nanos Valaoritis

BODY OF SUMMER

THE LAST shower was heard long ago
  On the ants and the lizards
Now the enormous sky is burning;
The fruits paint their lips
The pores of the earth open up slowly
And near the water that drips and mutters
A huge plant stares into the eyes of the sun.

On the upper sands who is he that lies
On his back and smokes the silver olive-leaves?
The cicadas warm in his ears
The ants toil on his breast
Lizards slide in the turf of his armpits,
And over his sea-weed feet gently rolls a wave
Sent by the little siren that sang.

Oh body of Summer naked and burnt
Eaten away by the olive oil and the salt
Body of the rock and shiver of the heart
Great waving of the osier's hair
Smell of basil over the pubic curls
Full of stars and pine needles
Body deep vessel of the Day!

The slow rains come, the sudden hailstorms
The earth drifts beaten in the blizzards claws
Which darkens in the deep with angry waves
The hills sink into the thick clusters of clouds

Yet from beyond you smile carefree
You recover your imperishable hour
As the sun meets you again on the sands
As the sky in your naked health.

SADNESS OF THE ÆGEAN

WHAT presence of soul in the halcyons of the afternoon
  What sea-calm in the voices of distant shores
The cuckoo in the garment of the trees
The secret moment at the fishermen's supper
The sea playing with an accordion
The distant longing of a woman
The lovely one that uncovered her breasts
When memory entered the nests
When lilacs sprinkled the west with fire.

On the caiques beneath the sails of a Madonna
They went under the guard of winds
The lovers of the lily's estrangement.
But how did the night babble the sleep to this point
With murmuring hair on the shining throats
Or on the great white shores
And how under the golden sword of Orion
Scattered and leapt high
Dust from the dreams of girls
With a smell of mint and basil.

On the cross-roads where stood the ancient witch
Setting the winds aflame with dry thyme
While the nimble shadows stepped lightly
Carrying a jug full of Silent Water
Easily they moved as though to enter paradise
And among the prayers of the crickets ticking across the plains
Wearing the skin of the moon the lovely ones came
To dance on the midnight threshing floor.

Oh, you omens crossing in the depths
Of the water which holds a mirror
And you the quiet glittering lilies.

57

When the sword of Orion returns
It will find under the lamp a poor man's bread
But the soul within the ashes of the stars
Shall find huge blended hands spreading to the infinite
And alovely sea-weed the last born of the shore
And years like green stones.

Oh, green stone—what storm-Seer saw you
Halting the light at the birth of day
The light at the birth of the world's two eyes.

Jules Supervielle

A CHILD OF THE HIGH SEAS

Translated from the French by Dorothy Baker

HOW WAS it made, this floating street? What sailors, with the aid of
what architects, had built it on the high Atlantic ocean, on the very
surface of the sea, above a gulf of some six thousand metres? This long
street of red brick houses, so discoloured now that they had taken on
a shade of French grey, these roofs of slate and tile, these humble, im-
mutable shops? And this spire with its lacy stonework? And here a
little patch containing nothing but sea-water, though evidently it was
intended for a garden, enclosed as it was by walls topped by bits of
broken bottle, over which occasionally a fish leapt?

How did all these things manage to keep upright, without ever being
washed away by the waves?

And this lonely, twelve-year-old child, who went in clogs and with
a firm step along the watery street, as though she were treading the
earth's hard surface? How did all this come about?

All these things I will explain to you in good time and insofar as I
myself understand them. And if, when all is said, some things still
remain a mystery, they will do so in spite of me.

Whenever a ship approached, even before it was perceptible on the
horizon, the child was seized with a great sleepiness and the village
disappeared completely beneath the waves. So no sailor, not even from
the end of a telescope, had ever set eyes on the village, nor even suspected
its existence.

The child thought she was the only little girl in the world. But did
she really know that she *was* a little girl?

She wasn't a very pretty child, because of her teeth that were rather
uneven and her nose a little too turned-up, but she had a very white
skin with a few gentle freckles on it. And her small person, dominated
by two grey eyes, rather shy but extremely luminous, sent through you,
from your body right to your soul, a sense of great wonderment, a
wonderment old and deep as time itself.

In the street, the only one of this little village, the child sometimes
looked to left or to right of her, as though expecting a light wave of

59

the hand or a nod of the head, some friendly sign of recognition. It was simply an impression she gave, without knowing it, for nothing and no-one could ever come to this lost village, always ready to swoon away beneath the waves.

What did she live on? From what she caught fishing, you may think? No, I don't think that was what she lived on. She found food in the cupboard of the kitchen safe, even found meat there, every two or three days. There were also potatoes, a few other vegetables, and occasionally an egg.

In the cupboards the food was constantly renewed. And though she took jam from the pot, the jam remained at the same level, as though things had one day been like that and must remain so evermore.

Every morning, at the baker's, half a pound of new bread, wrapped up in paper, awaited the child, on the marble counter behind which she had never seen any person, not even the hand nor the finger of one, pushing the bread towards her.

She got up early and raised the metal drop-shutters of the shops (here you could read *Public Bar* and there *Blacksmith, Modern Bakery* or *Draper*). She opened the shutters of all the houses, fastening them back carefully because of the strong seawind, and she left the windows open or closed according to the weather. In some of the kitchens she lit a fire, so that smoke arose above two or three of the roofs.

An hour before going to bed she began to close the shutters as though it were the most natural thing in the world, and she lowered the shop-shutters of corrugated iron.

The child carried out these tasks as though moved by some instinct, some daily inspiration that forced her to watch over everything. In fine weather she left a carpet hanging from an open window, or a piece of washing to dry, as though it were necessary at all costs for the village to preserve an inhabited air, to appear as life-like as possible.

And all the year round she had to take care of the flag on top of the little *mairie*, for it was much exposed to all weathers.

At night she lit the candles or sewed by the light of a lamp. Electricity had been installed in several of the houses, and the child switched on the lights gracefully and naturally. Once she put a crêpe bow on the doorknocker of one of the houses. She found that very nice. And it remained there for two or three days. Then she hid it.

Another time she found herself beginning to beat on the drum, the big drum of the village, as though to announce some piece of news. And she had a violent desire to cry out something that might be heard in every corner of the ocean, but her throat closed up and no sound came. She made such a desperate effort that her face and neck became almost black, like the face and neck of a drowned person. Then she had to put back the drum in its accustomed place, in the left-hand corner at the bottom end of the big room of the *mairie*.

The child mounted the steeple by a spiral staircase, its steps worn away by thousands of feet she had never seen. The steeple, which the child thought must have at least five thousand steps (there were really ninety-two) let in large slices of sky through its yellow, widely-spaced brickwork. And arriving at the top, she had to readjust the clock weights and wind up the clock with a crank, so that it would strike the hours truly, by day and by night.

The crypt, the altars, the stone saints giving their silent orders, all the chairs in good straight rows, and scarcely making a rustle, stood awaiting people of all ages; these altars where the gold had tarnished, would go on tarnishing through the ages; all these things both attracted and repelled the child, and she never entered the tall house, contenting herself in her hours of leisure by half-opening the padded door and snatching a brief glimpse of the interior, holding her breath as she did so.

In a trunk in her room were family papers; there were picture postcards from Dakar, from Rio de Janeiro and Hong-Kong; and they were signed *Charles* or *C. Lievens* and addressed to Steenvoorde (North). The child of the high seas knew nothing of this Charles and this Steenvoorde.

She had also, in a cupboard, a photograph album. One of the photographs showed a child that very much resembled the sea-child, and she often contemplated it with humility. It always seemed to her that the child in the photograph was the true, the right person; she was holding a hoop. The child had searched in all the houses of the village to find one like it. And one day she thought she had succeeded. It was the iron hoop of a barrel; but as soon as she began to bowl it along the sea-street, the hoop rolled wide and disappeared into the ocean.

In one photograph the little girl was standing between a man dressed as a sailor and a bony woman in her Sunday-best. The child of the sea, who had never seen man or woman, had long asked herself what these people meant, had even puzzled over this question in the depths of the night, when lucidity sometimes comes in a single flash, with the force of a lightning stroke.

Every morning, she went to the village school, with a great cardboard folder under her arm, in which she kept her exercise books, a grammar, an arithmetic, a history of France and a geography book.

She also possessed, edited by Gaston Bonnier, member of the Institute, Professor at the Sorbonne, and by Georges de Layens, laureate of the Academy of Sciences, a little herbal containing the most common plants, including both useful and harmful varieties; and the book was illustrated by eight hundred and ninety-eight drawings.

She read in its preface: 'During summer, nothing is easier than to procure in large quantities the plants of field and wood.'

And the history, the geography, the countries, the great men, the mountains, the rivers and the boundaries, how explain *them* to someone who knows nothing more than the empty street of a little village in the most solitary spot on all the wide ocean? But the sea itself, the sea which she saw marked on all the maps, did she even know she lived on it? She had once thought it possible, one day, just for one second. Then she had chased away the notion as dangerous and unwise.

At times, and with complete submission, she listened, then wrote a few words, listened again, then began writing once more, as though under dictation from an invisible schoolmistress. Then the child opened her grammar, and for a long time, her breath held, she bent over page 60, exercise CLXVIII, for this was the exercise she loved above all others. Here the grammar seemed to speak directly to the child of the high seas:

— *are you?* — *are you thinking?* — *are you speaking?* — *do you want?* — *must I appeal?* — *is it happening?* — *are they accusing?* — *are you capable?* — *are you guilty?* — *is it about?* — *are you keeping this present?* *Come,* — *are you complaining?*

(Replace the dashes by suitable interrogative pronouns, with or without the preposition.)

Sometimes the child felt an insistent desire to write down certain sentences. And she did so with great concentration. Here are a few of the sentences she wrote, chosen from a great many:

Let us share this, shall we?

Listen carefully! Sit down, don't move, I beg you.

If only I had a little snow from the high mountains, the day would pass more quickly.

Foam, foam that surrounds me, will you not one day become something hard and firm ?

To sing rounds, at least three people are needed.

There were two headless shadows walking along a dusty road.

Night, day; day, night; clouds and flying fish.

I thought I heard a noise, but it was only the noise of the sea.

At other times she wrote a letter, giving news of the little village and of herself. It was written to no-one, and when she ended it she sent her love to no person, and on the envelope there was no name.

And the letter finished, she threw it into the sea—not to get rid of it but because that was what she had to do with it—like those shipwrecked mariners, maybe, who leave in some desperate bottle their last message to the waves.

Time did not pass in the floating village. The child was always twelve years old. And it was in vain she stretched her small body in front of the wardrobe mirror in her bedroom. One day, tired of resembling the photograph in her album, with its wide forehead and plaits, she became vexed with herself and her portrait and spread her hair wildly about her shoulders, hoping that her age might thereby be violently and immediately changed. Or maybe the seas that surrounded her would bring some kind of transformation and she would see come out of them large goats with foaming beards, who would come near to her out of curiosity.

But the sea remained empty and the only visits she received were those of the shooting stars.

And then, one day, it was as though at last there was a change of destiny, a little crack in its firm purpose. A real, live cargo-boat, headstrong as a bull-dog and riding easily over the sea, even though lightly loaded (a lovely red band painted below her water-line gleamed in the sunlight)—a real, live cargo-boat passed along the sea-street of the village, and this time the village did not disappear nor was the young girl overcome by sleep.

It was exactly mid-day. The cargo-boat blew its siren, but the call of the siren did not mingle with the notes which struck from the steeple. Each sound preserved its independence.

The child, aware for the first time of a noise from the world of men, rushed to the window and cried out with all her might:

'Help! Help!',

and she threw her little black school pinafore in the direction of the boat.

The man at the helm did not even turn his head. And a sailor, with smoke coming out of his mouth, passed over the bridge as though nothing had happened. Others continued to do their washing, while on either side of the prow dolphins turned aside to make way for the cargo-boat which seemed to be in a hurry.

The little girl descended quickly into the street, lay down in the wake of the boat and embraced its tracks for such a long time that when she got up nothing was left but a stretch of immemorial and virgin sea. On going back to the house the child was amazed that she had cried 'Help!' She knew nothing at all of the word, only its very deepest meaning. And this meaning frightened her. Did the men not hear her voice? Were they blind and deaf, these sailors? Or were they more cruel than the depths of the sea?

Then a wave came to find her. This wave was extremely independent and had hitherto kept a distance from the village. It was a large wave and could spread out on either side much further than any other. In its crest it carried two seeming eyes of foam. It was as though it could

63

see and understand certain things, without always approving. Although it formed and broke many hundred times a day, it never forgot to furnish itself afresh with these two eyes, always set in exactly the same position and very life-like. Sometimes, when the wave's attention was taken by something interesting, it might be found resting for a whole minute together, its crest in the air, its function of wave that made it necessary to break and remake every seven seconds completely forgotten.

For a long time this wave had wanted to do something for the child, without exactly knowing what. The wave saw the cargo-boat sail off into the distance and understood very well the agony of the one who was left behind. Keeping aloof no longer, it drew the child a little way off, without any word being spoken, and as though leading her by the hand.

After kneeling in front of the child, in the manner of waves, and with the very greatest reverence, it rolled the child in its depths, pressed her there for one long moment, seeking, with the help of death, to snatch the child from her unhappiness. And to help the wave in this grave task, the child stopped breathing.

But the end did not come; so the wave threw the child high in the air, tossed her easily, as though she were no bigger than a sea-swallow, caught and recaught her like a ball, till she fell back at last among foam flakes big as the eggs of an ostrich.

At last, seeing that nothing could come of all this, that it could not succeed in bringing death to the child, the wave, in an immense murmur of tears and apologies, carried her back home.

And the little girl, who had suffered not a single scratch from this ordeal, began once more, without hope, to open and shut the shutters, and to disappear momentarily into the sea, as soon as the mast of a ship began to point towards the horizon.

Sailors who dream on the high seas, your elbows leaning on the taff-rail, beware of thinking too long, in the darkness and the night, of a beloved face. You might risk giving birth, in these places so essentially desolate, to a being that though endowed with human sensibility, cannot live or die or love, yet suffers as though living and loving and always on the point of death; a being most infinitely disinherited among those watery solitudes, like that child of the high seas conceived one day in the mind of Charles Lievens of Steenvoorde, a deckhand aboard the four-master *Le Hardi,* who having lost his twelve-year-old daughter during one of his voyages, had, one night, at a latitude of fifty-five degrees north and a longitude of thirty-five degrees west, thought of her for a long time and with terrible intensity, to the great unhappiness of that child.

Peter Yates

THE THEOLOGIC BIRD

(For Edith Sitwell)

... and in a dream I saw the Church like a great dark bird, and in
its beak was a pearl, and that pearl was the Word ...

WHO at the crossroads has not heard
The absolute and theologic bird
Cry out, relentless and oracular,
Yet known love's athlete joy, spectacular
Reclimb the slippery steps of Fall
In exaltation of the animal?

Or in each act where motives hide,
Felt snake of knowledge venomous with pride
Exhale the grief of falling in a sound:
A stinging hiss, Egyptian and profound,
Whose fullness has no utterance,
Yet is life's form, its stationary dance?

Satanic bird: with crashing of dark wings
It moves, inhales all sufferings
And lachrymose despair: invents the crux
Round which activity forever sucks
And leaves no wound, no disappearing trace
Of having been, no ugliness or grace.

Dark is the bird, and dark the magical
Black box on which its feathers fall;
And dark the horses on forever's road:
The sequin crown, the ghostly load
Of limbs exhausted by experience;
And dark the Word transformed by human sense.

E

An eagle's form! the rasp of wings
In midnight meditation, glitterings . . .
And we aspire to hear it speak;
Would know the end, tear from the iron beak
The faultless pearl by concentration formed,
Round which the early saints like drunkards swarmed.

Thought still consumes, gnaws at the eagle's claws;
And through the bird's unalterable laws,
And in the cursed condition of its flesh
We see the Word—pearl's vivid flash—
And all love's fate, immediate and far,
Ignites the cinder like a blazing star.

But every day it is more difficult
To choose: withstand the glowing cult
Of carnal pride: the goddesses of youth
Whose animal vibrations were a truth,
An intense beauty charged to exculpate
The world, and glorify the body's fate.

Dog howl and bone, the bitch of memory
Vociferous, and in the singing tree
Leaves vivid with corrupted yesterday . . .
The branches move; the thoughts like shadows play,
Dream of serenity, dream of the mind
Caught up, and dream of torture more refined . . .

Wheel of the world—September breathing charms
In exhalation—circle of white arms
And leaf in greenery, decay and fall:
Quintessence of the animal
Lithe in the grass, and in nocturnal flash
Divinity—pure rocket of the flesh!

But still a voice, a secretive command,
As though a statue raised a marble hand
And spoke: "from gross experience distil
The pearl . . . transfigure glory of the will
Through intense suffering, through nourishment
Of fitful glitter in life's excrement . . .

"And no escape! bathe in the air
Of cubic cities: ant-hills of despair
And brilliance where dark wings beat above
In mockery . . . or heat the bed of love
In knotted sexual hair, burn in the fire
The supple intuitions of desire . . .

"No human mouth, accomplice of your greed,
Can satisfy the immense need
You crave, or silence the splenetic bell
Of boredom's headache in nocturnal Hell
Where lust is mirrors, and the beds of silk
Spill morning rancour obvious as milk.

"Root up the stones: dissect the growing leaf;
From each minute particular of grief
Construct an image in the mind:
The lust of definition, undefined,
Disintegrates . . . becomes a flame
To lick identity and be the Name."

Shape of a god! rock in the wind
Immovable—derision of mankind,
And in the shifting dazzle of a sea
Thought sinks into its own identity,
Becomes the Form, the divine breath
And rainbow ether visible in death.

Yet too soon! years to be climbed like stairs,
And inescapable the will's despairs:
Ambition and the morbid pilgrimage
Of fame: nibs rusting on the whitened page,
And genius compelled by inward fire
To yield the symmetry of thought's desire.

And endlessly, beyond our sufferings
Reverberate the bird's dark wings—
Pearl in a vice! not to be grasped or known,
Incomprehensible by thought alone,
Till love's great wound, through which we see,
Exalts the Word in that captivity.

2

Edith Sitwell

SOME NOTES ON THE MAKING OF A POEM

I

WHAT ARE the processes in the making of a poem? It will not be believed by the Apôtres du Petit Bonheur, but the experience of the poet during the first processes of the inception and creation of a poem is, in its essence (I say this with all humility) akin to the experience and ecstasy of the saint.

'I am conscious,' said St. Augustine, 'of something within me that plays before my soul and is a light dancing in front of it; were this brought into steadiness and perfection in me, it would surely be eternal life.'

The firing in the soul is in many cases the same with poet and saint. In St. Bernard's *In Cantico*, Sermon 74, for instance, there is a mysterious passage which speaks of an experience like that of the poet.

'. . . the Word has sprung in me, and more than once: if It has entered frequently, I have not always been conscious of Its arrival. But I have felt It in me and I remember Its presence.

'Sometimes I have even felt the forerunning of Its entry. . . .

'Whence did It enter my soul? Whither did It return on leaving me? What is the place of Its entry? . . . It did not enter through the eyes, for It is not a colour; nor through the ears, for It is not a sound,[1] nor by the nostrils for It does not unite Itself to the air. . . . By what way, then, did It enter? Perhaps It did not enter, for It does not come from without, like an exterior thing.[2] Nor does It come from within, since Goodness, I know, is not in me.

'I mounted to the highest part of my Self, and higher still reigned the Word. Strange exploration, I descended to the depths of my Self,

---

[1] Here the experience of the saint and the poet differs. The word, for the poet, *does* come as a sound. But one from far away.

[2] Here again the experience of the saint and the poet differs. The material world has delivered up its essence to the visiting Angel.

and I perceived It in still lower depths. I looked outside: and saw It beyond all. I looked within: It was more close to me than my Self.'

Thinking of the phrase from ' The Marriage of Heaven and Hell ':

' *To create a little flower is the labour of ages* '

I ask myself if Blake was remembering the transcendental passage in Boehme's *The Aurora*, in which the Mystic saw and described the vision of the making of a flower. This passage—one of the most beautiful in all mystical writing,—though it is ostensibly about the forming, the growth, of a flower, might also be a simile of the processes of creation in a poet, of the coming together and embodying of the qualities that make a poem, of its gradual shaping and colouring.

Boehme saw the vision of the mingling of the ' astringent or harsh quality that is the heart, pith or kernel in the divine power, the contraction, compaction or imaging, forming or impression, the sour or attractive quality, the imaging or forming of all sorts of colours—with the " sweet quality," that of " the light, mollifying or softening ", and with " the bitter quality, the penetrating or triumphing which riseth up and triumpheth in the astringent quality and in the sweet ", " the cause of elevating joy, whence the life becometh stirring, and is well called Cor or the heart ".

' The astringent or sour quality is a body or source, which attracteth the sweet power, and the cold is the astringent or harsh quality making it dry.

' The sweet quality is the heart of the water, for it is thin and light and bright, and is like heaven: and the bitter quality maketh it separable or distinct . . .

' And when the sweet quality is dried, then it is like a corpus or body, which is perfect but wanteth reason.

' And the bitter quality penetrateth into the body, into the astringent or sour, and into the sweet qualities and formeth all sorts of colours.

' In the earth the heat of the sun kindleth the sweet quality of water, in all imaged or framed figures; and then through the heat the light cometh to be in the sweet water, and that enlighteneth the astringent or sour quality, and the bitter, so that they see in or by the light. . . .

' Now when the astringent or harsh and the bitter qualities get their light from the heat, then they see the sweet quality, and taste of the sweet water, and then they continually haste after the sweet water, and drink it up, for they are very hard, rough and thirsty, and the heat drieth them quite up. . . .

'And the sweet presseth vehemently from them . . . and hasteneth so fast, till a long stalk groweth up . . . and it (the sweet quality) leapeth, springing up through the astringent quality, and riseth up again aloft, so there cometh to be a hard knot in that place where the struggling was. . . .

'But when the sweet quality leapeth or springeth up through the knot, then the bitter quality had so much affected or wrought upon it that it was all in atrembling. And as soon as it cometh above the knot it suddenly stretcheth itself forth on all sides, striving to fly from the bitter quality, and in the trembling, leaping or springing up through the knot, it still gets more stalk or leaves . . . So when the heat from without thus presseth upon the stalk, then the qualities become kindled in the stalk, and press through the stalk, and so become affected or wrought upon in the external light of the sun, and generate colours in the stalk.

'And then the sweet quality yieldeth to be taken captive, and so the bitter, the sour, the sweet and the astringent reign jointly together, and the sweet stretcheth itself a little forth, but it can escape no more, for it is . . . caught. . . .

'And then from all the qualities which are in the body there groweth a bud or head.

'And then the sweet quality presseth forth in little leaves . . . or blossoms . . . '

This growth of the flower is strangely like the most secret processes of the poet's inspiration.

But what of the slightly later processes?

Dryden, perhaps, has conveyed the sense of these most clearly, in the Dedication to *The Rival Ladies*. He speaks of his work when it was still 'a confused mass of Thoughts tumbling over one another in the Dark: when the Fancy was yet in its first Work, moving the Sleeping Images of Things towards the Light, there to be distinguished, and then either chosen or rejected'.

I have spoken only of the secret spiritual processes of the poet. But what of his relationship to the outer world? These processes are of no use unless the spirit comes to be clothed with a beautiful and glowing flesh, the images of wonder given us by the world—they are of no use unless the inner heat of the earth is in their veins.

There is a great phrase in one of Meister Eckhart's Sermons (the Thirty-Ninth): 'Blood of the Holy Ghost and its glow is in one sense eternal, and in another temporal'.

Both body and spirit of the poem must have that holy glow.

What is poetry without fire?

Dr. Jung in *The Integration of the Personality* says ' In Heraclitus the soul at the highest level is fiery and dry '.

This should be true of the poet's spirit.

The purposes of poetry are many. Here is one:

Rimbaud in *Une Saison en Enfer* wrote ' *Devant plusiers hommes, je causai tout haut avec un moment de leurs autres vies.*'

It is this I would wish to do, I would wish to catch that fleeting moment of glory, that moment of the life men have banished, and to make it eternal for them.

But trying will not help me. Only patience. I must await that state of being I have known from time to time, ' the fiery driving or impulse of the spirit, that I can not resist or withstand, although the world always made a mock of me.'

II

THE SHADOW OF CAIN

This poem is about the gradual migration of mankind, after the second Fall of Man (the final separation of brother and brother, of Cain and Abel, of the rich and the poor) into the desert of the Cold, towards the final disaster, the first symbol of which fell on Hiroshima.

On the 10th of September, 1945, my brother Osbert and I were in the train on the way to Brighton where we were to give a reading. He leant across to me and handed me *The Times*, pointing to a paragraph in it, a description by an eye-witness of the horror of Hiroshima. . . . That witness had seen a totem pole of dust arise to the sun . . . a totem pole, the symbol of creation.

From that moment, night and day, the poem began. But it was not written until April of the following year.

The first two pages move partly on a physical, partly on a spiritual level. This perhaps is responsible for what may seem to some readers as a difficulty. So I will explain certain images.

The first line:

' *Under great yellow flags and banners of the ancient Cold* '

refers to the torn yellow heavens of the extreme cold.

But if I were to return once again to ' that which exists below the threshold of awareness . . . like a sun below the horizon ', (to quote Dr. Jung) I might remember—but it would be a memory I had allowed to sink to a great depth, far below my ordinary consciousness—that the hair of Judas was, according to legend, yellow, and that he has often been painted in a yellow dress. I should have a dim memory, too, of a vision of the silent advance of terrible yellow banners of Asian hordes in a vast desert. . . . And from that memory I should come to the fact that I have noticed how like the faces of the Chinese are our faces in the extreme cold . . . yellowed, mysterious. . . .

But these memories dwell with the Sun below the horizon.

And the poem occurs in no particular place, until it moves to Hiroshima. It would be dwarfed by a human space. Hiroshima is no longer that: it has taken a third place beside Heaven and Hell.

> 'But the Cold is the highest mathematical Idea . . . the Cold is Zero—
> The Nothing from which arose
> All Being and all variation . . . It is the sound too high for our hearing,
>   the Point that flows
> Till it becomes the line of Time . . . an endless positing
> Of Nothing, or the Ideal that tries to burgeon
> Into Reality . . .'

Here the physical state and the spiritual state are fused.

> ' The Cold is the highest mathematical Idea, the Cold is Zero . . . '

This refers to the feeling one has in the most intense cold that all material things are abolished, all is reduced to Nothingness, to a desert, to Zero. There are no longer boundaries. . . .

Zero is the highest mathematical idea, Lorenz Oken said.

In this present state of the world Man is almost reduced to complete bareness,—to the bareness of all but the Central Point . . . the bone, the small spark of the spirit. . . . All else is gone. But the theorists, the experimenters who believe that from such reduction to Nothingness a new Civilization, the betterment of Mankind, will arise, see in this complete destitution, hope.

> ' It is the sound too high for our hearing '

the intense cold has always seemed to me to have an affinity with an unheard sound—with the sound that is too high for our hearing.

> ' And now in memory of great oscillations
> In temperature in that epoch of the Cold
> We found a continent of turquoise vast as Asia
> In the yellowing airs of the Cold: the tooth of a mammoth,
> And there, in a gulf, a dark pine-sword

'To show there had once been warmth and the gulf-stream
in our veins
Where only the Chaos of the Antarctic Pole
Or the peace of its atonic coldness reigns.'

In Sir Charles Lyall's *Geology*, there is a description of the finding of a mammoth's tooth, with a pine leaf (symbol that there had once been warmth) hidden in a crevice. He speaks too of the variations in temperature in that early stage of the world's history.

> *'And when we reached an open door*
> *The Fate said " My feet ache ".*
> *The Wanderers said " Our hearts ache ".*
>
> *There was great lightning*
> *In flashes coming to us over the floor:*
> *The Whiteness of the Bread*
> *The Whiteness of the Dead*
> *The Whiteness of the Claw—*
> *All this coming to us in flashes through the open door.'*

I dreamed those lines, about two months before I began the poem, and woke up saying them to myself. But when I dreamed it, the first line began:

> *'And when we reached the open door.'*

The door was then, as I dreamed it, the door of birth. And the three lightnings are three out of the five primal realities.

As I used the symbol in this poem, the open door is, roughly, one to which Fate has led the Wanderers,—a door through which one must find one's own path. The three lightnings are still those three primal realities.

> *'In the streets of the City of Cain there were great Rainbows*
> *Of emeralds: the young people, crossing and meeting.'*

—the young people, the hope of the world, after the terrible flood and the Ice Age.

> *'We did not heed the Cloud in the Heavens shaped like the hand*
> *Of Man . . .*
> *. . . the Primal Matter*
> *Was broken, the womb from which all life began.*
> *Then to the murdered Sun a totem pole of dust arose in memory of Man.'*

To my utter amazement two critics, writing benevolently about this poem were obviously unaware that this verse and those succeeding it refer to the dropping of the Atomic Bomb.

> ' And in that hollow lay the body of our brother
> Lazarus, upheaved from the world's tomb.
> He lay in that great Death like the gold in the husk
> Of the world . . . and round him, like spent lightnings, lay the Ore—
> the balm for the world's sore.
>
> . . . .
>
> And to that hollow sea
> The civilization of the Maimed, and, too, Life's lepers, came
> As once to Christ near the Sea of Galilee.
>
> They brought the Aeons of Blindness and the Night
> Of the World, crying to him " Lazarus, give us sight".
> O you whose sores are of gold, who are the new Light
> Of the World! '

Lazarus, the Poor Man . . . Poverty, now moved into a new tomb of gold,—exposed for the first time to our sight. Lazarus, the symbol of the new earthly resurrection of Man, that is to be brought about by the new experiments. Lazarus, the hero of death and the mud—taking the place in men's minds of the Hero Who was born in a Manger.

> ' They brought to the Tomb
> The condemned of Man, who wear as stigmata from the womb
> The depression of the skull as in the lesser
> Beasts of Prey, the marks of Ape and Dog,
> The canine and lemurine muscle . . . the pitiable, the terrible,
> The loveless, whose deformities arose
> Before their birth, or from a betrayal by the gold wheat-ear.'

—a description, this, of the physical signs of prenatally disposed criminals. Among my multitudinous notes for this poem, there is this line:

' These with their insensibility, their disvulnerability ' quoted from Havelock Ellis—then comes this note:

' Dr. Olivier speaks of the healthiness of eyes in criminals . . . presenting a picture that is almost identical to the one seen during infantile existence.'

Alas! Alas!

That picture is too terrible. Rather ' the Aeons of Blindness ', far from that innocent Paradise.

Rex Warner

THE POETRY OF GEORGE SEFERIS

THERE is no land and sea so haunted with gods and heroes as the
land and sea of Greece. Indeed there is something disturbing and
oppressive as well as inspiring in the thought of such a weight and variety
of history, such a radio-activity of the divine. The mountains may stand
for a moment clear and distinct, the sea may glitter in ' innumerable
laughter ', rock and tree and building may be outlined in a heavenly
peace against the purest of skies; yet one has only to move a few yards,
there need be only the slightest change in the weather, and the whole
scene is transformed into something wholly different that is still wholly
Greek. The Greek land-and-seascape, in its clarity and its mystery, its
brilliance and its terror, in its stability and in its hurrying movement,
in all its contradiction is still the best basis for attempting to understand
the Greek genius. For it must be admitted that most academic views of
the Greeks are either incomplete or mistaken. The distinction between
the ' ancient ' and the ' modern ' Greeks is positively harmful, since it
disguises the most obvious facts that the ancient Greeks were modern
and that the modern Greeks are ancient. Moreover, who are supposed
to be ' the ancient Greeks '? The men of Marathon? Long before
Marathon the Greek seas were full of ships. Small bands of sailors from
insignificant but individual towns were opening up the Black Sea,
founding Marseilles, colonising Sicily and sacking Troy. And as important to the Greek and European spirit as the Parthenon are the vast
rock structures of Mycenæ, the palace dripping with the blood of
kindred slain by kindred, the wealth and savagery of the house of Atreus.
Or, when we speak of ' ancient Greece ' are we thinking merely of
Athens and the Ionian cities from which our arts and sciences began?
If so, we are forgetting the wholly different cultures of Sparta and of
Crete and of a hundred jealously independent towns and islands. There
is the army, mostly from obscure states, that, under Xenophon and
Cheirisophos, defied the Great King at his gates. Then there is Macedonia,
the diffusion of Greek culture to the banks of the Indus, ' glories ' to
quote Seferis, ' buried in the depths of Asia '. There is the intellectual
conquest of the Romans by the Greeks, and its brilliant results, the
barbarian invasions (always an element in the history of this beautiful

and tortured land), the long splendour of Byzantium, whose armies guarded civilisation and whose intellectuals defined law and dogma. There are centuries of dispersion and of oppression. There is never a weakening in vitality. There are the Wars of Independence, the legends of Byron and of Navarino, the heroism of the island navies, the massacres and the intrigues.

There is a new nation with a new literature and an intense consciousness of its regained freedom, dating in its present form, from a mere hundred years or so back. The newness is important, and yet how can such a nation not be conscious of its unique, tremendous, glorious and tragic past?

To be conscious of such a past may well mean to be overwhelmed by it, and there are certainly many Greeks who, perhaps because the weight of it all is too heavy for them, seem to try to free themselves from one or more of their great traditions and to imagine as a basis for their thought or art either only the classical age, only Byzantium or only some modern movement. To feel the whole of the past is a task which is certainly beyond the power of most people, and for a Greek poet the task is extraordinarily difficult.

In a way the Greek language itself is symbolical of the poet's difficulties. In its three thousand years of known history it has shown a vitality and a persistence which are quite without parallel, except possibly in the language of China. Yet with this tremendous vitality there has always been variety and sometimes fluidity. This language has been in critical periods of the world's history both dominant and pervasive. The language of two or three generations of writers in a city state much smaller than Birmingham has dominated the thought of Europe ever since. The same language, common in the Middle East, made possible the diffusion of Christianity and kept civilisation alive in Byzantium. The language changed, but it kept its quality and its individuality. Today writers in Greek, who have all discarded the puristic tongue which attempted an artificial stabilisation of a living language, can draw on a vocabulary which has the longest tradition of any in Europe and which has also perhaps the strongest local associations. A word may carry one back three thousand years to Homer or it may be one that reflects the Cretan Renaissance or a Macedonian village of today. So complex, so vital is the very vocabulary with which a Greek poet has to deal. There are a hundred Greeces, and they are all Greek.

One of the reasons for the eminence of George Seferis is the fact that he is always conscious both of the depth and of the variety of his tradition. He is conscious too that in the Greek tradition there is now to be incorporated another tradition, that of the rest of Europe, which, though descended from the Greek, has developed along different lines.

A brief outline of his life will indicate how well he is qualified to feel and to understand not only his own country but the problems of Europe as well. Yet, since a bare recital of events in a man's life means little without some knowledge of the man himself, it may be well to attempt some description of Seferis today.

There is a photograph, taken, I think, by George Katsimbalis, that great talker and untiring critic to whom Greek literature and the Greek language owe so much, which shows Seferis, with his large head and great bulk, emerging, with a slight smile and a critical eye, from between two massive drums of a prostrate and broken column. That photograph is characteristic. I think of him too swimming in the sea like a great whale with massive sloping shoulders, or walking with a slight stoop, his big head thrust slightly forward, his large but quick eyes darting suddenly to some object which would have escaped the notice of others. Indeed one is at first surprised by the quickness in contradiction to his considerable weight, by the intellectual alertness which suddenly flashes into those large deep eyes, which, when they are in repose, call to mind some biblical figure of speech,—pools or wells or cisterns. Melancholy indeed he looks very often, perhaps when late at night, in some open-air café, over an ice or a cup of coffee, he is speaking of the general situation of literature or recalling events in Greek history. But his melancholy is always giving place to his own individual and charming humour. He has written limericks in Greek; he has made a strange collection of natural sculpture from old roots washed up on the shore of the island of Porus; he carves grotesque shapes on the handles of walking sticks. Both his conduct and his conversation are unpredictable, yet they are marked always by simplicity, energy, courtesy and charm. One knows him first as a poet and a diplomat, but cannot know him long without knowing him as a friend.

The places of his birth and education have much to do with his intense feeling for the Greeks and his deep knowledge of contemporary Europe. He was born in the year 1900 in what was then the Greek city of Smyrna, a city rich and prosperous, conscious of forming part of the Greek world. Seferis learned no Turkish at school, and indeed, when a few hours of the language became compulsory, would take to the sea with his friends and leave school for the day. His childhood was greatly influenced by the holidays he spent at a little sea-port along the coast, which was the ancient Clazomenae. Here in conversations with fishermen and peasants, in view of the chains of islands and the sea, he learnt of the depth and extent and variety of Greece, whose sailors had voyaged and settled from Spain to Colchis, from Egypt to Cilicia. And at Smyrna itself there were monuments of ancient and Byzantine ages, so that the present was vivid and the past not unreal. Even today, Seferis says, a fisherman seems to him to speak with more authority than a cabinet minister.

The first world war, dated for most countries from 1914 to 1918, was for Greece virtually a ten years war, from 1912 to 1922. Already in 1912 the young Seferis had been excited by the Greek victories against the Turks. In 1914 he left Smyrna for Athens where he studied in a secondary school till 1917. One can imagine the impact which must have been made on his mind not only by the beauty and sanctity and brilliance of the place, but by the fact that here he was in the capital of a free Greece.

From Athens, after four years, he went to Paris where he studied law and literature from 1918 to 1924. This is a most important period in his life for two reasons. It was in Paris that he first, in these formative years, became fully acquainted with French literature and with European thought. Among the moderns Proust, Gide and Valéry were the names discussed. Seferis was also keenly interested in the symbolist movement and in Jules la Forgue, a fact which has a bearing on his later interest in T. S. Eliot. At the time he knew little of English, though in 1924 he visited England for the first time, carrying with him a pocket edition of the text of *Hamlet* with a French translation. He still treasures the volume, though it was not of any great assistance to him on this occasion.

The other element in his life during these years, which I have mentioned as particularly important, was the news of the Greek disaster in 1922 and of the exodus of the Greeks from Asia Minor. Seferis was in exile, but as he heard the news,—of how, for example, the terrace of his mother's flat in Athens had been used to shelter fifty homeless refugees, —he knew that the world of his childhood had been shattered. Perhaps it was this experience which accounts for that element, so prominent in his work, of the sheer agony of being and feeling oneself to be a Greek, —brilliant, fearless, energetic, with nerves taut for action, but, like Orestes, pursued by Furies.

In 1925 Seferis returned to an Athens whose population had been vastly swollen by refugees. In the following year he entered the Foreign Office and his first appointment abroad was, in 1931, London, where till 1934, he worked as Vice-Consul and as Acting Consul General. During this period, in a city so different from Athens, he came across in a book shop a copy of T. S. Eliot's short poem *Marina*. It enchanted him, partly because it recalled to him the Mediterranean, and partly because he had found a poet who seemed to be working along lines similar to his own.

For in 1931 his own first book of poems, 'Στροφή' (*The Turning Point*) had been published. The critics found in it what English critics had found in Eliot's early work, a new blend of conscious discipline with a modernity that often seemed to the conventional outrageous. Indeed Seferis and the poets who followed him were, like Eliot in England, reacting against a sort of ' Georgian ' style and were basing their startling innovations on a close and affectionate study of the past. It is notable that one of the earliest admirers of the work of Seferis was the old poet Palamas, who declared that *The Turning Point* was indeed a turning point, the sudden beginning of a new movement in Greek literature.

In the spring of 1934 Seferis returned to Athens, and in the following year published his second volume of poems *Mythistorema*. In this volume he ceases to use the conventional rhythms and metres of Greek poetry. He has more to say and he says it in a looser form of verse, though ' loose ' is not a word that is at all appropriate to his style. He is one of those who express passionate feeling with the utmost restraint and contrives this partly by the use of symbols and partly by a deliberate avoidance of any superfluous word. Adjectives are used sparingly. The simplest words appear in a complicated context.

Those years in Athens were prolific. *Gymnopedia* appeared in 1936 and other poems in the following year. In 1936 also he published a translation, with a commentary, of Eliot's poems.

From 1937 to 1938 he worked as Consul in Albania, and in 1938 came back to Athens to act as liaison with the foreign press. During this period he made friends with a number of young English writers in Greece. A description of him and of his friend George Katsimbalis may be found also in Henry Miller's book *The Colossus of Maroussi*. But the days of gaiety, somewhat hysterically described by the American author, were not to last, and none knew this better than Seferis. After the brilliant victories of the Albanian campaign came the German invasion. On the 6th April, 1941, the day of the German onslaught, Seferis, speaking for the Greek government at a Press Conference, said: ' We know now that there is a new order in Europe. We know its meaning. We know that it means the assassination of the weak; it means the employment of the basest forms of lying to carry out these murders; it means the systematic extermination of small nations.'

Later in the same month, on St. George's Day, he left for Crete with the Greek government, and, driven out of Crete by the German invasion, went, first to Cairo and then to South Africa where, for some time, he was First Secretary at the Embassy in Pretoria. It was the second time that he had lost his country and his possessions.

Exactly a year after his arrival in Crete he returned to Cairo, again as liaison with the press. He was in Egypt during the dark days of Rommel's advance to Alexandria and for the dawn of victory at El Alamein in 1943. Next year he returned to the Ministry of Foreign Affairs, working in London, in Cairo and in Italy, and in October came back from exile to Athens. Like every other patriotic Greek he felt the tragedy of the civil war in December. In May 1945 he became Chef du Cabinet to the Regent, Archbishop Damaskinos, a post which he held till the restoration of the Monarchy in 1946.

During these years of disturbance, exile and tragedy he had continued to write. Volumes of poetry appeared in Athens in 1940 and in Cairo in 1944. One of these, a beautifully produced book, contains the most charmingly gay and ironical illustrations by the author.

I have used so many words to describe, though briefly enough, the events of Seferis' life, because those events help to explain why he is specifically a Greek poet and yet different from other Greek poets who are known to English readers. He has, for instance, none of the prophetic style of Sikelianos, a style which, if Sikelianos was a less great poet, would be rhetorical. He has not the clear feeling for sunlight and enjoyment that one finds in Elytis. Both these poets might be called, though in different ways, ' typically Greek '. Yet Greece, this narrow, bounded and restricted land, contains an infinity of aspects and lives on a tremendous depth of experience. Seferis, with his sensitive and critical mind (a combination which in our times seems to be becoming rarer) is constantly aware of the complexity of what meets the eye. His style, though far from cautious, is certainly premeditated. He draws on many sources, from Homer and Aeschylus to Erotokritos, to the literature of France, to Cavafi, Palamas, Yeats and Eliot. Like these last he is acutely conscious of the contemporary situation, having seen much of ' the systematic extermination of small nations ', of the slogans which replace thought, of the violence and intolerance which lie so close beneath the diseased skin.

There is nothing mystical in Seferis' approach to his problems and here he differs profoundly from Eliot. Yet perhaps, after all, he is affected by something which might be described as a different form of mysticism, a mysticism of history and tradition rather than of philosophy or religion. There are no barbaric explosions of hysteria in his feeling for the Greeks; the knowledge of tragedy and of responsibility is too great for that. It is perhaps because Seferis is so much a European that he is so aware of being Greek. He uses the names of Greek towns and islands with a reverence or with an access of feeling, as Eliot uses terms of theology. Behind the brilliant and varied landscape, in the centre of the seas that ' blossom with corpses ', in the voyages of adventurous men, in local customs, in massacres and in exile is the meaning which he looks for, and the close sincerity of his search is in itself an illumination.

NOTE

In what I have written I am very greatly indebted first to George Seferis himself, and then, like everyone else who has studied Greek poetry, to our mutual friend George Katsimbalis who, with his enthusiasm and his fine critical sense, has more than anyone living, helped foreigners to understand and to appreciate the beauties of modern Greek literature.

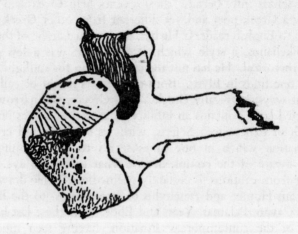

Osbert Sitwell

A SHORT CHARACTER OF
ARNOLD BENNETT

THE READER will have noticed for himself how many of the friends described in my book,* I first met through the good offices of Robert Ross. It is impossible to overrate his eager promotion of the interests of young writers in whom he believed, to exaggerate the trouble he took, the tact he expended. With him friendship was a solvent, which united every friend with every other. Nor, so long as he lived, were there any quarrels, at any rate in this body, though he possessed several enemies of the most bitter sort, chiefly, of course, as the result of his innumerable kindnesses in the past. But he possessed no foes among the young, and several poets of my generation, notably Sassoon, Robert Graves, Wilfred Owen, Robert Nichols, and my sister and myself had reason to be grateful to him. His wit, for which he was justly celebrated, was apt to die with the day that gave it birth, being of the type that, most exquisite of ephemerids, is so true and pointed as to depend for its value on the currents, trends, and feeling almost of a particular week. A few *mots* survive, to hibernate in the mind, and come out again on an early summer day: and these, no matter if you disagree with the opinion they express, are brilliant. His tact—even when, as in the example I give, it was mock-heroic—aided his manner, and his voice, with its slight transatlantic roll of the ' r ', left from a Canadian childhood, produced a mollifying effect and exercise to a powerful charm. He took me, in this instance, to luncheon with a hostess of the time, who was said to have a negro strain in her. Inadvertently, I remarked about somebody, during the course of luncheon, ' His energy is said to be due to black blood.' Robbie kicked my foot under the table, and remarked in an innocent voice that was at once reproving to me and calming to others, ' Not *black* blood, Osbert: Senegalese, Senegalese! ' . . . All this, however, gives little impression, I fear, of his kindness, wit, humour, or the warmth of his personality: little idea, either, of the sound of his rather purring voice, or the intoxicatingly subversive element in his conversation, in its refusal to accept other people's rags and tags of ideas, the implicit attack on authority—an element in all wit—combined with a

* This is part of Volume V of Sir Osbert Sitwell's reminiscences *Left Hand, Right Hand*.

curious care, sincere but mock-deferential, for the surviving Victorian conventions. To many of us, he acted as impresario, reaping no benefit for himself thereby: he got our poems published, encouraged the notice of them in the press and by the public, introduced us to older and more eminent writers whom he thought would be likely to be interested in our work, and to be of use to us. . . . It was in this fashion, and under Robbie's auspices, indeed almost under his command, that I first made the acquaintance of Arnold Bennett.

Our meeting took place in the marble-lined hall of The Reform Club, an architectural monument so impressive—obsolete as the Collosseum— as to seem to clamour already for time to unroof it, and allow the winds to race through its wide arcaded galleries and pompous marbled corridors, and at the same time to sum up England, so that, as my brother remarked to me, it seems the ideal background for the opening of a novel by Jules Verne; the place, for example, where two club-Englishmen would give breakfast to an eager young French inventor about to set forth on a perilous journey, the first ever to be made of its kind; it was here, then, that the meeting took place, in the spring of 1918. Robert Ross had, of course, invited me to meet the famous man at luncheon because he was one of the pontiffs of literature: in this similar to, though in all else different from, Gosse who, like Agag, walked delicately through the antique pastures of literature, culling the flowers; whereas Arnold Bennett was devoted to the present, and constituted to the readers of his age a living reminder that a great novelist—for such they considered him— could exist in others, beside the Victorian reign, and could at the same time be—what no great Victorian had achieved—the best paid journalist of any epoch. (I forget now what Arnold Bennett was said to be paid for a word—can it have been 2s. 6d. or 5s. ?—but in any case, I know that when, many years ago, I was threatened with a libel action about a short story which had been published in a book of mine, and was advised to settle out of court, I computed that this had been the most expensive story ever written—though in this case to the author and not the publishers —because I had been obliged to pay out more per word than ever Arnold Bennett earned.) At the time of which I talk, he was, as well, one of the directing heads of British War Propaganda, under the press-barons; in fact every young author had to be presented to him, in the same way that every tourist in Rome must be taken to see St. Peter's. To sum up, he was a great figure of the epoch, the successor and heir, it seemed to many, of Charles Dickens; a famous publicist. His novels, his short stories, his literary criticism had won the respect of the middle classes in England and America, and were widely read throughout the English-speaking world; his reputation stood high in France and Germany. In America, he had enjoyed the greatest personal success of any visiting writer for fifty years. And his diaries, even today, reflect the people and spirit of the day with a singular and vivid faithfulness. Fifteen years after an author's death is the most difficult time at which to estimate correctly the contribution he has made: but whatever may be the ultimate importance or the reverse of Arnold Bennett, he cannot be omitted from any, even rather fragmentary survey of the literary and social scene of the 1920's, and just before and after. Moreover, I am not here concerned with him *as* a writer—though at the same time the fact that he was one accounts for his appearing in this essay—but as a person.

Even in spring days, the hall of the Reform, full of the funeral pomps of Liberalism, crowded with marble frockcoats of the 1840's (a period in which Liberators were as common in England as they are abroad today), haunted by these heavy, white, side-whiskered ghosts of Prosperity no less than by the more enticing shade of Soyer—who accomplished, in fact, so much more practical good for humanity than some of the originals of these Carrara images—is chilly, full of fog, though outside the boughs are breaking into green spray, and the soft winds blow. But we had only a moment to wait, for on the very stroke of one, Robbie's other and chief guest materialised. Hedged off, as he was, with the laurels and bays of twenty seasons of fame, I felt a little frightened of him. And his physical presence, which combined that of a Midlands business man with the rather solid panache of a great *French* novelist—the Parisian world-novelist of the mid-nineteenth century, with a touch, more than a touch of Balzac, and a reminder, here and there, of Dumas the Elder, and of Emile Zola—did nothing to diminish it. His greying hair, his tired eyes—in which the expression of his often remarkable kindness could not at once be read—his corpulent habit of body, natural both to the vigour of his type and to a sedentary way of life (it was only in the last decade of his career that a desire to be more elegant, to be more ordinary in his manner of pleasing, or perhaps a sudden drop in his self-confidence, asserted itself and was responsible for a decrease in the volume of his figure) placed him a whole generation ahead of me, and made him seem—though I was, it is true, then only twenty-five—further removed in age than actually he was, in a manner in which one never felt my dear host, Robert Ross, to be distant. (But Robbie one knew, and saw at once, could understand and share the feelings of the young; would, indeed, never know any other.) Nor can it be pretended that Arnold was an attractive or imposing, although he was a prosperous-looking, middle-aged man: his blunted, yet rather sharp and inquisitive nose, his bristly, grey moustache and slightly protruding teeth, his creased, sallow face and recessive, dented chin, produced a far from handsome effect. I was puzzled, too, at first, by his fob of jingling gold seals and his coif of grey hair, which seemed to me—or would have seemed, if I had not gone in some awe of him—to be pretentious. Then, in an opposite, more naive direction, I catalogued, for a final reckoning of character and attributes, a gold toothpick.

All these personal adjuncts, however, were in reality only another expression of the manner in which he liked to think things out, of the pleasure he derived from the everyday details of existence; clothes, food, walks, and the decoration of his rooms. As one grew to know him better, one began to comprehend the breadth of his intelligent and informed joy in life. Moreover, just as I have, elsewhere in this book, mentioned that a pineapple, rising like a palm tree from a handsome dish in the centre of his dinner-table, constituted to him a visible emblem of his fortune, and that the shadows of poverty, which had in early days surrounded him, had been at last securely dispelled, so, I think, every time he regarded himself in a glass, and saw the grey upstanding lock in the middle, above his forehead, his elaborate waistcoat and his seals, it brought home to him not only the same comforting assurance, but told him, too, that he now cut a figure in the world as one of the most famous of living novelists. Certainly, he liked looking in mirrors, and one could often, as he passed them, see him preen himself and observe his own reflection. Of this trait, I can give the following illustration. A great friend of his told me that he had been to call on Arnold, who had just moved—in January 1923—into a grander house, 75 Cadogan Square. The new owner had, however, at once been struck down with influenza, and his friend found him in bed, recovering. Noticing that the walls were hung with large mirrors, and that Arnold, lying propped up on pillows, and still looking excessively ill, was gazing contentedly at the repetitive perspective of images of himself thus afforded, his friend remarked:

' I couldn't lie there, looking at myself reflected, on and on into infinity like that! '

To which Arnold replied, in a tone of complacency:

' I . . . t suits me down to the ground! '

Though I was not present when these words were said, I can as I write them hear in them the exact tone and run of his voice; his voice which was so typical and easy to mimic. At first his always intractable and often outrageous stammer rendered me nervous for—and, therefore, of—him. But, again, as one got to know him better, it became clear that his remarks gained, actually, in force and quality from the way in which his hesitation, so irksome to himself, obliged him to regulate his utterance, gearing it to various speeds, one or two slow words, then two or three fast, or a few slow, and then a run of fast, to get them in before the stammer caught him again. This physical drawback had forced on him a style of conversation that, like his voice, still rather rough, and retaining the broad, flat Midland ' a ', as in *Flax*, proved peculiarly suited to apophthegm and plain, nutty speech, such as when he said to me one day:

' The most important thing for a young writer is to write his stuff; the next is to know where to place it.'

Or, when, after a well-known female novelist had been discussed, he announced:

' As a writer, there's . . . only-one-thing-wrong-about-that-girl,' (pause) ' she can't . . . write! '

Or his verdict on a painter and writer, now growing elderly, whom, at first, I, like members of many succeeding generations, had thought an entertaining character and talker; so entertaining that I had spoken of him much to Arnold, and had arranged to bring him to tea in George Street (this was in about 1920). At last, the day came. I took my brilliant friend there, but his customary essays in truculence Arnold treated with a genial indifference, and, as soon as he said goodbye, and left the room, remarked:

' That man's a . . . *bore!* '

Or, to take a fourth instance, his warning to my sister. She had been saying how low she rated the writings of an author whom I had lately named Middleton Moral, when Arnold interrupted her and said:

' Spiritual pride is a terrible thing, Edith. Remember whatever you may think of my work, or I of yours, or both of Moral's, on the Judgment Day it will appear to the Almighty as pretty-much-the-same-thing.'

His stammer, too, gave point to his enjoyment of a joke, whether his own or someone else's, for he would stammer also in his laughter, his face would grow a red-brown and he would laugh yet more.

On the first day I had met him, Arnold had been particularly tired, and his hesitation had been severe, indeed agonising—for it varied greatly —to witness. He had kept on, as was his wont occasionally, at all times, but, especially when it was extreme, throwing back his head, with his mouth a little open and with a look of troubled persistence in his eyes, and beating his knee with a regular rhythm, until at last he could get his words out: this being done, perhaps, not only to help himself, but also to lessen the suspense for those in his company who waited for him to speak. All the same, it gave the onlooker an uneasy suspicion that he might be disliked for being present when such a display of control was necessary: for many stammerers, on the days when their affliction is at its most severe, bear an involuntary grudge against their companions. But in Arnold Bennett's case it became plain in time that he bore no ill will. . . . The conversation, though, had lagged. Arnold watched me with his shrewd, sharp gaze; to which was added the attentive, side-long glance of the stammerer, in its origin due no doubt to his wish to see how others are bearing the strain of his prolonged struggle for words. Robbie took the burden of the talk on himself, just as, with his generosity of spirit, he assumed many other loads. However, I talked a good deal myself, for I am one of those whom an intense silence renders loquacious, anxious to do anything to prevent the coming of the inevitable silence that will never be broken: and so, I had improvised a grievance which really I had hardly felt or had time to feel; the fact that the younger writers possessed no journal in which to vent their opinions or publish the writings of those whom they admired. Poetry, in those days, especially, was a Closed Shop; to which admission was only gained through friendship with the leaders or secretary, and, of course, by a firm adherence to the bird-loving tenets of the day. The mention of a blackbird or thrush in a poem meant you were a safe man, unlikely to give trouble, to the Union. It was necessary also to take an interest in cricket. . . . Well, all this was true, odd as it may sound a generation later: but I was aware that on this topic I was saying more than I meant, talking too much, too vehemently, too wildly. . . . I do not know how my host felt about it—he was probably too tired, after his efforts, to consider the matter—but myself, I was conscious as I left the Reform, both of failure and of exhaustion, for Bennett, it seemed to me had hardly troubled to say goodbye.

It can be imagined then with what intense surprise I received a letter from him, the next morning, asking me to have luncheon with him alone, at a restaurant, early the following week, to discuss a matter of business. I could not think what it could be. . . . The day came, I arrived at the restaurant, and found my host waiting for me. No sooner had we sat down at a table than he asked:

'Did you mean what you said about wanting a paper for young writers?'

I said, yes, I had meant it.

There followed a glazed pause, in which he looked at me dully. Then he continued:

'If you'll edit it, I'm willing to back it.' And proceeded at once, in the most business-like way possible, to make arrangements for putting the plan into execution. 'I'll give you a letter to take to Chatto & Windus. They've one great advantage over every other publisher: they've got a man with a first-class brain working there, Frank Swinnerton. He's a great friend of mine, and will fix it up for you.'

In all truth, I was taken aback: for, as in some fairy stories, my careless wish had been granted too rapidly, almost before being formulated. I had not, until the luncheon I had mentioned, even contemplated editing a paper—after all, the War continued, and I was still in the Army—and so I was unprepared; my ideas were in chaos. However, I went the next day, and many times subsequently, to see Swinnerton; for Arnold insisted always that, if anything needed to be arranged it should be done in proper, workmanlike fashion. The firm of Chatto & Windus, then in St. Martin's

Lane, made a great impression on me, for it was the first publishers' establishment I had ever visited. A long dark passage stretched from the office, into which the door opened, to a distant nucleus of inner shrines, unbelievably remote and sacred, and to which, I think, I was never, in the course of the next few years, allowed to penetrate: while, on the way between the office and these sanctuaries, in the straight, dark and narrow corridor was a number of doors, which led into small, airless dens, intensely small and confined, lit only by artificial light, and lined with books: closets which, as if to remove the feeling of claustrophobia that must assail anyone immured in one of them, were all open at the top, but above the level of the head, so that you could hear the conversations but could not see the talkers. These cramped boxes always seemed to me to be full of waiting figures, hopeless aspirants for literary fame; but sometimes, as I walked down the passage on entering or leaving, I would see the face of a friend, and the tall, lank figure of Aldous Huxley or Lytton Strachey (two of ' Chatto's authors ', for in such slavish terms do we talk) would elongate itself up through an open door, as if expelled therefrom by the pressure of space, in the manner—if such a contradictory yet accurate image be permissible—of a rather languid jack-in-the-box.

Though a good deal accrued eventually to my benefit through these visits, and through my several interviews with Frank Swinnerton, nothing came of them immediately. The project fell through, or, more accurately, fused itself with another: partly because I was still in the Grenadiers, and could not guarantee the time in which to edit a monthly magazine (and Arnold believed in a monthly journal, and would have nothing to do with a quarterly) and partly because, in the end, the backing proved unnecessary, since, as I have elsewhere explained, Frank Rutter was at the time looking for two editors to help him to revive a quarterly called *Art and Letters,* and offered one post to Herbert Read, and one to me.*
But leaving these circumstances out of account, I fear that my lack of business habits, and the fact that, out of consideration for him, I purposely refrained from continually plaguing him about the paper although I had originally broached the matter, rather riled Arnold; who must have thought that I manifested, not only a certain dilatoriness, but a lack of interest.

Nothing, I said, came of the project directly—but still the amazing offer had been made; an affirmation of faith in young writers, and an effort—unparalleled to my knowledge in its generosity—to help them at the cost of a considerable personal sacrifice; for Arnold, having been poor, liked money and knew the value of it. It was, moreover, through these meetings with Swinnerton, and perhaps, even, through

* We both of us accepted, and continued to edit it for some two years. Some account of this venture will be found in the forthcoming fourth volume of my autobiography.

Arnold's more personal intervention, I do not know—that my first book of poems, *Argonaut and Juggernaut*, was published by Chatto's the following year. Several writers of my generation, painters and musicians (for he was interested in all the arts), must owe Bennett a similar debt. I record all this, because it is, in its essence, very typical of the character of a man who was seldom in his lifetime or afterwards given credit for possessing, as he did in an extreme degree, the quality these facts display: indeed, to the contrary, I have often heard it stated about him in conversation, by those who must have known him very slightly, that he was penurious. I, on the other hand, know of many instances of what can only be termed discriminating munificence on his part: notably one in which he sent for a celebrated younger writer, in whose judgment he had faith, and said to him:

'Look here! I've made more money than I expected this year: here's a cheque for five hundred pounds, for you to give away, as you think best, to younger writers and painters: there's only one condition; my name must not be mentioned in connection with it.'

Moreover, he was as unsparing of his time as of his money: many of us used to consult him on numerous matters, and he would always find the necessary half-hour in which to see us, though he liked to run his day's programme to the fraction of a second. In the same way, if one wrote to ask him his advice on any point, he always answered promptly, and in a manner that proved he had given every consideration to the subject. Thus I remember consulting him by letter from Amalfi, some years subsequently, on which was the best literary agent to handle my writings, and on general lines of policy, and receiving an invaluable, and indeed masterly, letter of counsel in reply.

Above all, Arnold Bennett rated such qualities as punctuality and personal competence. He preferred geniuses who could look after themselves to those who had to be looked after. He endured and even seemed to enjoy the company of business men, and to cherish a high respect for the makers of great fortunes and especially the holders of newspaper power. The name of Lord Beaverbrook, for instance, appeared to exercise a kind of spell over him. He liked people to lead tidy, punctual lives. His flats or houses he wished to be well run, and in the terms of the house-agent, well-appointed. In addition they were always furnished with his own individual taste, handsome and to some extent original, influenced by a love of colour, and of objects of solid worth. He believed in regular stretches of work, long walks and early hours. In the years after 1923, when he moved from George Street to Cadogan Square, I used often, from the top of a 'bus, to espy him crowned with a bowler hat, a prosperous and somehow important figure, in a trance of thought, walking below through the crowded King's Road, or further afield. But, he told me, there were two kinds of walks he took, one to solve the problems with which the plots of his books presented him; the other, when he looked about him, to gather ideas, or to take in the atmosphere of a given neighbourhood. And, concerning the hours he kept, when I first knew him, and he and Marguerite Bennett were living in their large flat in George Street, for large dinner parties, a notice, placed on the chimney-piece, would proclaim to the possible recalcitrant the ineluctable hint ' *Carriages,* 10.45 '. It may be that his reasonableness, whether innate or acquired, sometimes betrayed him: for he believed that with the application of intelligence and the exercise of forethought, everything in human life could be regulated; whereas no doubt in the end he discovered that certain human faculties, attributes, emotions, stand altogether beyond the scope of common-sense control.

After the first two encounters I have described, and although my failure as a man of practical affairs may have a little chagrined him, we never-theless quickly became friends, and during the dozen years or so that followed, until his death in 1931, I saw much of him. Equally, my brother and sister delighted in his company. I do not remember how soon our friendship had ripened, but in 1919 he wrote to me, in answer to a letter in which, as I thought was fitting to an older and famous man, I had addressed him as ' *dear Mr. Arnold Bennett*',

' *Dear Osbert, call me dear Bennett, dear Arnold Bennett, dear Arnold, dear Uncle Arnold, or anything you damned well like, but never again call me " dear Mr. Arnold Bennett".*
' *Your affectionate Uncle,*
' *Arnold.'*

After receiving this, we always called him Uncle Arnold, and wrote to him in that style, and though, as I have said earlier, he had seemed, when first one met him, to be older than he was, in the years that followed one was continually surprised by his youthfulness, by—for example—his interest in the other arts. At the age of about sixty, he actually *liked* new ideas. About pictures, he knew a good deal: very much more than most authors; perhaps because, in addition to a natural feeling for painting, he had lived much in Paris, where writers pay attention to it. He numbered many musicians among his friends; he gave a magnificent party, I remember, in his house in Cadogan Square for Ravel, and he took an interest in the careers of young English musicians and conductors, such as Eugene Goossens. When, however, he played the piano himself, which occasionally he did, the effect was not happy. I have heard him play in George Street, classical duets with Lady Ross;* and I recall my

* Lady Ross was the wife of Professor Sir Denison Ross, for many years head of the School of Oriental Languages.

sister saying to me that the light clatter of their fingers on the keys exactly reminded her of the sentence said to be posed in schools where aspirates were taught as a test of pronunciation:

' *Hens' hooves hitting the hard high road.*'

He was, however, an accomplished water-colourist, and I have in my collection a water-colour of his, representing a convent in Portugal, which he gave me on his return from a visit to that country in 1920.

Youthful, again, was his sense of humour. It had no primness about it, as had that of the other pontiffs, and retained, in spite of the kindness of his nature, a certain inherent ferocity, which, for example, enabled him to enter into the spirit of the doings and sayings of my sister, brother and myself, apparently often incomprehensible to others of his age. This, I think, is manifest in what he wrote about us in August 1923, in *The Adelphi*: for it was a time when we were giving, and receiving, no quarter. My second volume of poems was rejected by Chatto & Windus, and accepted by Grant Richards, and it was this book he was reviewing.

' *Osbert's* OUT OF THE FLAME,' he wrote, ' *is the longest stride forward by the Sitwells up to date. It made me reflect that the trio is still quite young, and may develop in astonishing ways. It really excited me; for in my short-sightedness I had looked upon Osbert as simply a satirist. . . . And lo! he is now creating ideal beauty. . . .*' But the portion of what he wrote which shows, I think, a certain enjoyment in our exploits, runs:

' *The Sitwells can all write. . . . Further, the Sitwells are all personages. Further, they all afflict the public—I mean the poetic public—which is a grand thing to do. . . . They exalt in a scrap. Battle is in the curve of their nostrils. They issue forth from their bright pavilions and demand trouble. And few spectacles are more touching than their gentle, quiet, surprised, ruthless demeanour when they get it, as they generally do.*'

To return to his youthful enjoyment of jokes and of fun, and to his high spirits, he records in a letter,* dated 12.1.20:

' *I have begun to work again, and my health is much better. The mere thought of going to Portugal has had a marvellous effect. Strange! We went to the Olympia Victory Circus on Saturday night with the brothers Sitwell. It was a great thing. Especially the roundabouts. We came home with the brougham full of hydrogen balloons, which occasionally swept out on their strings through the windows into the infinite ether . . .*'

---

* From Arnold Bennett's *Letters to his Nephew, Richard Bennett*. Messrs. Heinemann published this book, with a short preface by Frank Swinnerton, in 1936.

How well I recall that occasion! The party consisted of Arnold and Marguerite Bennett, Aldous and Maria Huxley, and Sacheverell and me. It was a night of bitter cold and deep snow, and the vast iron enclosure, within which the circus ring had imposed an attempt at form, was full of light yellow fog, splintered by arc-lamps, and further darkened by peat dust; among which the Fratellini—it was the first time I had seen these famous Spanish clowns—tumbled, cried, and disciplined an imitation baby. The balloons, too, straining at the leash were new to me, and a delight: as was Arnold's almost school-boy pleasure in them. And I recollect his amusement, because they gave me an inspiration, and I outlined to him, for he always took an interest in my father, a new scheme; similarly to fill my father's invariable companion, a round air-cushion, shaped like a life-buoy, so that, just as that dignified, bearded gentleman was going to sit on it, in his accustomed place in the Reading-Room of the British Museum, it would either soar with him, aloft, as the eagle once carried Ganymede to Olympus, or, eluding him, would go bumping up to the ceiling by itself. . . . So, on parting, we piled the balloons into Arnold's brougham, and watched them drive away, through the snow, into the fog, a balloon every moment bobbing out of the window, until, quite soon, the vehicle was lost to sight.

It was after his return from the visit to Portugal to which he alludes at the beginning of the letter I have quoted, that he gave me the water-colour I have mentioned: in return for presents that my brother and I had brought him from Spain the previous year: two genuine sombreros, one brown, one black. He had seized on them, as we had thought he would, with delight, though they required a degree of courage to wear, for they would have appeared unusual in any country except that of their origin. They carried immensely large, stiff brims, in a perfect circle, and stiff crowns, too, tapering gradually to the top, and had leather straps which fastened tightly under the chin. I have no doubt that he wore them, for to do so would have been part of his fun. He took the greatest trouble over his appearance, went to the best tailor, and imported shirts— his shirts were always a delight to his friends—from the most famous of Parisian shirt-makers. To behold him, however, at his finest, most typical, one had to see him in full evening dress—preferably at a first-night. Yet I do not think his reflection in the glass afforded so intense a realist any illusions concerning his exterior; he saw too straight for that.

Just as children sometimes stand, without terror, in the very path of tigers, and are alleged to be thereby preserved from danger, because the beasts admire a display of so much courage, so, too, Arnold remained resolutely unafraid when confronted with new ideas or their promoters. And it was for this reason that, when Sacheverell and I organised in August the first exhibition of modern painting of the Paris School to be held in London since the outbreak of war in 1914, we asked Arnold to write the preface for it. In addition, we had hoped—of course, vainly—that the position he held with the public, and his admirable common sense, might suffice to quiet the outburst of popular rage that would undoubtedly otherwise ensue at the sight of a few modern masterpieces. The two Post-Impressionist Exhibitions at the Grafton Galleries should have stood as a warning to the crowd: but no! Though Arnold wrote in the foreword . . . ' *It is the first exhibition of its kind since the war, and the best of its kind since the celebrated exhibition at the Grafton many years ago* . . . ', the public would not accept his hint, and albeit the famous writer publicly tipped them the work of Modigliani as a winner (this was the first time his paintings had been publicly exhibited in London), yet did the heathen roar, rave and, after prowling around the galleries, howl together in the newspapers. The result—one which they would have understood—was that they lost the chance of a valuable investment. On my advice, I am glad to say, Arnold bought—he says in his diary for fifty pounds, but I believe it to have been for sixty—a very beautiful reclining nude by Modigliani: that which I considered the finest picture in the exhibition. He notes in his *Journal* for August 1929:

' *Eight years ago I bought a portrait of a woman by Modigliani—certainly one of the greatest painters of this century—for £50. So that when I received an invitation to a private view of Modiglianis in a West End Gallery, I** *accepted it at once. There were no fifty pound items in this show. I halted before the picture which pleased me most, and asked the price of it. The Manager replied "A Paris dealer offered me £6,000, but I refused it . . . "* '

Arnold himself, in the great slump shortly afterwards, parted with his own Modigliani at a huge profit.

That indeed, was as it should be. I need hardly say that this man, accused so often of avarice and stinginess, this writer, the most highly paid of his epoch and the continual victim of overwork, had accepted to write the preface—and no one except a fellow author can estimate the nuisance value of having to break off what you are working at, in order to write something else, however small it may be—without payment of any kind, solely in order to help two young writers in whom he believed, and whom he knew to be undergoing a difficult time financially. But, in truth, there was always something big and generous about him, just as there was about his physical personality, even though it may not have been prepossessing at first sight, a delightful quality of exuberance; which in itself plainly proclaimed him to be no skinflint. In London or Venice or Paris, in great world or little, he remained always, as the result of the

* *Journal*, 1929. Arnold Bennett. Cassell, London, 1930.

94

conditions of his early life, that happiest of beings, a provincial on holiday; a comfortable provincial of genius on holiday. This accounted for his interest in large hotels (all business men from the provinces enjoy a similar Babylonish thrill when they arrive at a famous place of fashion or luxury), for his attention to clothes and innumerable other details of life. He still dared to take nothing for granted, but was in no sense uneasy: yet this verdict must be modified, for he was naturally at home with the arts. As he grew older, there was no shrinking of his spirit, as sometimes there is. One night, in the last months of Arnold's life, I dined in Chiltern Court with H. G. Wells, who occupied a flat in the same block, a few floors down, and only half the size of that into which his contemporary, friend, and rival for fame had lately moved. The talk turning on his neighbour, a reflective look came into H. G.'s eyes, and he remarked in a confiding tone, and his very personal voice, so characteristic in the way it went high and low: ' The trouble is, whenever I do a thing, Arnold does it too, but twice as posh.'

John Lehmann

THE MAN WHO LEARNT TO WALK NAKED

LIKE ALL the poets of my generation, I have worshipped at the shrine of W. B. Yeats. I fell heavily for *The Lake Isle of Innisfree* when I was a small boy at my private school; and I have gone on reading him with devotion ever since, poems, plays, *Autobiographies*, but always the poems above all. No wonder, then, that the few occasions on which I was privileged to see him, or hear him speak, have remained in my memory as pictures with a special glow and holiness. The last occasion I remember particularly clearly; it was in a London club, a year or two before the war, and he was sitting in the middle of the huge pillared drawing-room, alone, with a book in his lap. He was not reading the book, because he had fallen asleep; but even in this rather unexpected impromptu nap he looked, to me, very noble and very romantic, as if he must be dreaming of Cuchulain, and the cloths of heaven, and the wild swans at Coole. Oddly enough, however, owing to some previous train of thought I have long since forgotten, it was his lines to an Irish airman that came into my mind:

> *Nor law, nor duty bade me fight,*
> *Nor public men, nor cheering crowds,*
> *A lonely impulse of delight*
> *Drove to this tumult in the clouds. . . .*

And it struck me then, as it still strikes me now, that what was so impressive about him was that he too, in his own poet's way, had been true all his life to a ' lonely impulse of delight ', and in an age about as inimical to such a faith as any one can find in history. In his very first volume, in 1889, he had announced, striking something a little more sincere than the fashionable attitudes of the day, in the poem called *The Song of the Happy Shepherd*, that ' words alone are certain good '; and through all the artistic and political movements with which he came to be associated that idea remained his lodestone. He did not cut himself off from the clamour and violence and passionate partisanship that resulted in his country's independence, but he never let those things shout down the voice of poetry inside him. Other poets have taken to prose, or public affairs because their ambitions could not be satisfied with the small fame such a lonely calling could bring them, or because they were not strong enough, or convinced enough about the ultimate worth of poetry to swim against the stream; but the springs of Yeats's inspiration remained unmuddied through dangers that a great contemporary of his thought only exile could ward off; and what is even more significant, they never dried up. A dedication so unwavering—and at the same time so success-ful—is almost without parallel in our distracted times.

It is, of course, this faith in poetry, and the continuity of his expression of it, that has made Yeats so powerful an influence on the younger poets who began writing during the last twenty years. But to say that is only to state a remarkable fact in its most general terms; and the attraction has been so magically strong, that anyone who wants to understand the meaning and action of poetry in the sum total of life must try to examine it a little more closely.

If one reads through the sequence of Yeats's poetry, from the beginning with *Crossways* to *The King of the Great Clock Tower* and the final poems before his death, one is bound to recognise that his start was so brilliant, that if he had only been known by his first two volumes, if he had died fifty years ago after the publication of *The Rose*, he would still have been outstanding and would still have been quoted and represented in every anthology today; but that what made him so dominating a figure, is that he went on living and his art went on developing, both in its technical mastery and in its content. He has summed up that development himself, in his own inimitably pithy way:

> I made my songs a coat
> Covered with embroideries
> Out of old mythologies
> From heel to throat;
> But the fools caught it,
> Wore it in the world's eyes
> As though they'd wrought it.
> Song, let them take it,
> For there's more enterprise
> In walking naked.

Like some other great artists, he disconcerted his followers by aban-doning his early manner just when they had made themselves proficient copyists of it, and the wonderful embroideries he fished up from the deep chest of Irish legend and ancient myth, and refashioned with a craft learnt from the pre-Raphaelites and symbolists, but already entirely his own in the early nineties, he abandoned for that ' walking naked ' which is the chief miracle of the phase which followed the 1914 war. It was not enough simply to live on; other poets have lived into middle and old age, and left their art way behind them in the tomb; but by growing as an artist as well he achieved what so many young Romantics have been denied by death, what Chatterton and Shelley and Keats a hundred years before and the poets of the 1914 war in his own time could only promise. And by his amazingly complete flowering he preserved his early work in all its freshness, for such lyrical masterpieces as *Innisfree* and *Wandering Aengus*, which might by themselves have seemed cloying to a latter-day taste, acquire a new interest, a new life when related to *Meditations in Time of Civil War* and *Coole and Ballylee*, becoming part of a crown of achievement greater than any of its individual jewels. All the cunning he had learnt in his craft as a young man, all the intensity of dream which made the visions of the Irish renaissance pass into the artistic consciousness of the modern world, were reborn into a new wisdom, a maturity of heart and mind enriched by the experience not merely of the cycle of love, but of public affairs, of contact with many men of many kinds that the theatre, and war, and revolution on his doorstep brought him. William Wordsworth is probably the very last poet in the world the sumptuous embroideries of *Crossways* and *The Rose* would call to mind; and yet it is precisely the Wordsworth who wrote the famous Sonnets of 1802 that I am reminded of when I read such a poem by the mature Yeats as *Nineteen Hundred and Nineteen*:

> *We too had many pretty toys when young:*
> *A law indifferent to blame or praise,*
> *To bribe or threat; habits that made old wrong*
> *Melt down, as it were wax in the Sun's rays;*
> *Public opinion ripening for so long*
> *We thought it would outlive all future days.*
> *O what fine thought we had because we thought*
> *That the worst rogues and rascals had died out. . . .*

One may believe that Wordsworth, in the final reckoning, is the greater poetic phenomenon; and yet it is apposite to remember that the author of the *Ode on Intimations of Immortality* showed no such continuity of growth and harvest, and that by the time he had reached the age when Yeats wrote *Byzantium* he had become an almost unreadable old bore.

This evolution then, the way in which the young Romantic who began by singing of ' eternal beauty wandering on her way ' while Kipling was thumping out his tunes for Tommy Atkins, learnt to transpose his marvellous music into another key, and present us with a symbol-figure of a poet whose ivory tower of dreams became the real tower from which he could hear the cry of ' Vengeance for Jacques Molay ',— this maturing into Delphic utterance is one of the chief sources of his power over the minds of contemporary poets. But behind it all, of course, was the supreme craftsmanship, compounded of so many elements which one is apt to overlook as one enjoys the effortless richness of his lines. Yeats had the great advantage of starting with a special territory of his own, the woods and mountains and wild shores where Fergus and Cuchulain and Niamh celebrated their loves and sorrows and heroic battles, and the singer was forever in quest of 'the red rose-bordered hem'; but he could never have established his claim to this territory so success-fully if he had not, as all great poets before him, invented his own music, his own recognisable voice as a poet, almost from the beginning. It is not easy to define exactly how a poet performs this essential act of crea-tion: it is a matter partly of the manipulation of vowels and consonants,— and some of Yeats's most famous poems, such as *Innisfree*, have been analysed to show his astonishing mastery of this side of his craft; it is also partly a matter of the rhythms that are woven across the regular metrical beat of the line, which give such individuality to the attentive ear that a quatrain of four-beat lines by Yeats could never be mistaken for one by Blake, or Hopkins or Eliot; equally important is the choice of vocabulary, the extent to which archaic or poetic words are associated with more current or colloquial words, latinate words with Anglo-Saxon words, monosyllables with polysyllables. Look, for instance, at the way he introduces a truculent word like ' supersession ' into one of his shortest and best-known poems:

> Nor dread nor hope attend
> A dying animal;
> A man awaits his end
> Dreading and hoping all;
> Many times he died,
> Many times rose again.
> A great man in his pride
> Confronting murderous men
> Casts derision upon
> Supersession of breath;
> He knows death to the bone—
> Man has created death.

In all these things, Yeats very rapidly established his own, immediately identifiable manner, and though his skill increased as he grew older— if we except perhaps a period just before the 1914 war when he seemed to be marking time,—it is the same quality that attracts us in the last poems he wrote as in *The Sorrow of Love* or *The Song of Wandering Aengus*. He was particularly successful in overcoming what seems to be the chief stumbling-block of so many modern poets, the assimilation of the technical and apparently unpoetical word into his verse; and as he began to drop the 'embroideries out of old mythologies' and turn more and more to the concrete world of contemporary Ireland, he showed that he did not have to limit his range, as an exquisite minor poet like Ernest Dowson did in his own generation, in order to avoid producing the lumpy and indigestible porridge that has been offered so often and so hopefully in the last twenty years in the guise of honeydew and the milk of Paradise. He transfigured the colloquial, as Eliot has in his own very different way. The *Meditation in Time of Civil War* provides many examples of this power of his, none more striking than the section called *The Road at My Door*:

> An affable irregular
> A heavily-built Falstaffian man,
> Comes cracking jokes of civil war
> As though to die by gunshot were
> The finest play under the sun. . . .

And who but Yeats could have succeeded in that opening section of the poem called *Ancestral Houses*, which is conceived in the grand manner if ever a poem was, in concluding a stanza so easily, so conversationally, as with the lines:

> And maybe the great-grandson of that house,
> For all its bronze and marble's but a mouse.

All these elements I have separated from Yeats's craftsmanship, the way vowels and consonants are handled, the counterpointing and cross-rhythms, the choice and mixture of vocabulary, are, I think, important in the final make-up of his individual music; but the *Meditation in Time of Civil War* brings us up against what was, perhaps, in his later manner at least, the supreme secret of style: I can only call it the tone of voice. It derives from all of them, but it is at the same time something more than their sum total, a quality as elusive as the quality which makes one man a brilliant speaker in public or on the air, and another, of otherwise equal—or greater—gifts, a failure; the final endowment which decides whether posterity will cherish a poet, or not. I do not believe it can be analysed any more than any of the other supreme secrets of genius, though even the most cunning imitator will immediately reveal that he has not got it. It is almost the whole secret of those terse little gnomic poems which Yeats delighted in as he grew older, the culminating example being the 'Words for Music Perhaps', whose creation, after a long illness, Yeats has described himself in that memorable passage of the notes to his *Collected Poems*: 'Then in the spring of 1929 life returned as an impression of the uncontrollable energy and daring of the great creators; it seemed that but for journalism and criticism, all that evasion and explanation, the world would be torn in pieces.'

One of the most precious gifts of the greatest poets has always been their power of concentrated expression: of making even quite a short lyric or ode carry as much 'criticism of life', or imaginative refinement of experience, as a prose-writer can often pack into a novel or a playwright into the three acts of an evening performance, so that through one particular experience or set of images a great range of other experiences is suggested, and a few dozen lines seem to extend this radiation almost infinitely. If I were asked whether I would feel more deprived and starved of spiritual food by the loss of the hundred best novels I could name or the hundred best poems, I would unhesitatingly reply that I could more easily spare the novels. And among the hundred, I would certainly include several examples from the poetry of our own time, which have just this density and power of radiation, and from Yeats's last period, among the first. What is so amazing is that this 'sixty-year-old smiling public man', as he described himself in *Among Schoolchildren*, could write poems of such imaginative splendour and intellectual richness as *Coole and Ballylee, Byzantium, Sailing to Byzantium, The Second Coming* and *Meru*, transforming his early myth-making magic into a magic more completely his own and even more potent after a lifetime of consistent integrity and achievement, so that the poet who has cast off the old mythologies and learnt to walk naked appears at the end in the new, less fancifully but even more superbly embroidered robes of the prophet-philosopher. We may discount much of the neo-platonism and the hints of the occult, as we may discount much of the speculation on time in T. S. Eliot's later work, but the residue of visionary poetry is so tremendous that we can easily accept the playing with theories as the necessary scaffolding for a mind which had long before rejected conventional religion, and whose work derives much of its intensity from the search for a substitute—from the attempt to make high poetry itself take its place:

> *Another emblem there! That stormy white*
> *But seems a concentration of the sky;*
> *And, like the soul, it sails into the sight*
> *And in the morning's gone, no man knows why;*

And is so lovely that it sets to right
What knowledge or its lack had set awry,
So arrogantly pure, a child might think
It can be murdered with a spot of ink. . . .

It may be that, almost unconsciously, today's generation is fascinated by the aristocratic note in Yeats's poetry, that quality in his make-up which brought him to his well-known eccentric political sympathies, but represents something that is rapidly vanishing from our world and is regretted ever more deeply as it vanishes; nevertheless, it is, I think, finally, the prophetic and visionary power of his last work that completes his sway over the poets who have followed him. And as civilisation staggers, as in the climax of a drunken dance, from the rape of Poland to Belsen, and from Belsen to Hiroshima, and so on to the unimaginable horrors of the future, Yeats's famous vision of the 'rough beast' that 'slouches towards Bethlehem to be born' while

Turning and turning in the widening gyre
The falcon cannot hear the falconer;
Things fall apart, the centre cannot hold. . . .

with its wonderful catching-up and modulation of Shelley's words in *Prometheus Unbound*, can only appear more and more ominously apposite to an appalled world that seems incapable of averting the birth. And the sibylline master does not only see what is swelling in the womb of time more truly than all the politicians, economists and Frankenstein-fiddlers in their laboratories, but admits us also for dazzling moments into that air of eternity the gates of which only poets can unlock, when we know that civilisation, our civilisation like all those which have preceded it,

. . . is hooped together, brought
Under a rule, under the semblance of peace
By manifold illusion, but man's life is thought
And he, despite its terror, cannot cease
Ravening, raging and uprooting that he may come
Into the desolation of reality:
Egypt and Greece good-bye, and good-bye Rome.

* * *

3

Bernard Denvir

MODERN FRENCH TAPESTRIES

THE MASTERPIECES of European painting are but so many pieces of plaster, wood, or canvas on the surface of which smears have been made with pigments, forming a pattern of shape and colour, but analysable, eventually, into the last indignities of chemical formulæ, yielding their secrets to the omniscience of modern technology. There has been no limit set to the variety of these marks, and the pressure of technical limitations has been slight. The sculptor is bound to the exigencies of stone, the engraver to the particularities of his medium, but the painter is free within the confines of his canvas. That is his major problem. With tapestry, a form of expression relegated all too frequently to the obscure anonymity of 'the decorative arts', an intermediate stage is reached. The artist's vision emerges from the wool or silk with which it is identifiable; it is no thin skin of delight, stretched across a fustian background, but is created from within its medium, a kind of midway state between bas-relief and painting.

The resemblance to painting is, in some ways, unfortunate, for we are ever ready to seek a criterion of familiarity with which to judge the unfamiliar, and in the pilgrimage of pleasure through the French tapestries at South Kensington we were ever on the outlook for a family resemblance, catching here a hint of Veronese, there a reminiscence of Cézanne. But the relationship between the loom and the easel is not a simple one, and it is an error to praise, or to blame Oudry for popularising the idea that a tapestry should look like a painting. The creations of Oudry, of Boucher and of Perrot were intended to form part of a larger decorative scheme, and it was that which determined their nature, not the desire to ape 'les grandes machines'. Boucher's tapestries are more delicate than his paintings, and few artists could hope to rival the 14,600 tints which the Gobelins could use for one hanging. 'The Apocalypse of Angers' had managed with twenty-five.

The most convincing argument adduced by those who look upon the tapestry of the eighteenth century as verging upon decadence is the blight which it cast over the nineteenth century. In the exhibition there is nothing to cover the gap between J.-B. Huet's ' Pastorales' woven a few years before the Revolution, and Gromaire's ' The Seasons', woven during the Occupation. Not all the pomp and circumstance of the First or Second Empires produced a tapestry worthy of the name, and the looms at the Gobelins, Beauvais and Aubusson turned out an endless series of dreary imitations of designs which even in their original conception had been more than a little jejune.

Painting in the meantime had been carrying on its disinterested quest for reality of one sort or another, and it was obvious enough that the atmospheric realism of the Impressionists could never have been woven in wool or silk, even had the demand existed. Tapestry has always been a more social art than painting, for it involves a fairly complicated commercial process, and France never produced a William Morris who would endeavour to invest a private æsthetic Odyssey with all the glamour of a cultural mass-migration. With Cézanne, however, the need for structural discipline became explicit in painting, and from that time modern tapestry became a possibility, to be realised as soon as contemporary painting had attracted contemporary prestige. The ' Nabis', influenced by Gauguin and the teachings of Sérusier at the Académie Jullian, tried to bring some order into the wild enthusiasm of Impressionist fervour, and Bonnard, who was of their number, was one of the first to make essays at transferring his compositions to tapestry. Already there was some hint that the limitations of medium might provide a suitable check on the unlicensed vagaries of individual fantasy, but there was not yet a strong enough background of popular interest. The Atélier Flandrin at Grenoble made some attempts at modern tapestries in 1915, and in 1920 Dufy was commissioned to do a hanging for Beauvais, but it was found that the process would be too expensive.

It was not until 1933, when Madame Cuttoli started her work, that the general implications of an art form, almost providentially designed for the school of Paris, were fully realised. It is unfortunate that none of the early attempts were to be seen at the London exhibition; one was faced with the final accomplishment of the revival, without being allowed to see the stages whereby it was reached. In the original exhibition, as shown in the Musée Moderne at Paris, there were some eighty modern tapestries; at the Victoria and Albert there were only thirty-eight, and none of these show the application of tapestry to the adornment of furniture. Some, however, may remember the exhibition of Madame Cuttoli's collection which was held at a London gallery in 1937. Only the works of Lurçat and Miro had been specially visualised in terms of cartons for tapestry, but even the mere reproductions of paintings which composed the contributions of the other artists showed how easily modern painting could adapt itself to the dictates of the warp and the woof.

COUTAUD

Modern French Tapestry

JEAN LURÇAT

Modern French Tapestry (1946): JEAN PICART LE DOUX

The Sawn Log

MICHAEL ROTHENSTEIN

Bridge End, Essex

Gethsemane (1944)

MICHAEL AYRTON

Winter Drought (1944)

Entrance to a Wood

MICHAEL AYRTON

The Great Yews of Odstock (1944)

Boy and Window (1947)

[Reid and Lefevre

JOHN MINTON

Cornish Landscape (1945)

[Coll.: Hollis S. Baker, Esq.

The Gale-swept Orchard (1946)

KEITH VAUGHAN

In the Orchard (1946)

JOHN MINTON: *Thames—View from South Bank* (1946)

KEITH VAUGHAN: *Workmen with Weather-vane* (1945)

The contrasting textures of Picasso's 'Inspiration' and the liturgical sanctity of Rouault's 'La Sainte Face' were further extensions of their creators' artistic personalities.

Although there were none of these in the present exhibition, some idea of their effect could be obtained from the work of Savin, who allows his purely pictorial prejudices to overcome any temptation he may experience to hedge his expression around with too cautious a regard for a different medium. He is concerned with a large heroic vision of the life of rural France, and the massive figures of peasants collect their apples, beat their walnuts and celebrate in their vineyards with the unselfconscious grace of their ancestors in the 'Très Riches Heures du Duc de Berry'. A tapestry cannot exaggerate; by its very nature it is saved from the utmost excesses of abstraction or Surrealism, and achieves a certain simplicity of comprehension, almost in spite of itself.

It is doubtful how far the movement would have gone, however, had it not been for Lurçat. His first interest in tapestry was awakened during the war of 1914–18, and for twenty years he immersed himself in the traditions of the craft, experimenting, exploring and codifying. He discovered that vegetable dyes are better than chemical ones, that the range of colours can advantageously be reduced to fifty and that the future of tapestry is inextricably linked up with its past. Guillaume Janneau, the Director of the Mobilier National, helped and encouraged him, and an Aubusson industrialist, François Tabard, also took an interest in the movement. In 1939 an exhibition of contemporary tapestry was held at the Petit Palais, and in the same year the Ministry of Fine Arts sent Lurçat, Gromaire and Dubreuil to organise a full range of activity at Aubusson. On the day that Petain signed the armistice with Germany the society of 'Peintres professionels de Paris, cartonniers de Tapisserie' was founded with Dubreuil, Lurçat, Gromaire, Valentine Prax, Coutaud, Dufy and two architects, André Lurçat and Louis Rollin.

All the tapestries in the modern section at the exhibition were woven during or since the war, and more successfully perhaps than anything else, they offer surety for the continuance of French culture. No other country in the world could have provided so convincing a solution to the very real problem of combining the great traditions of humanist art with the communal preoccupations of today. These tapestries are not ornaments to adorn the externals of life; they are not 'decorative' in the sense that a wall-paper is; they are living entities, experiences rather than comments on experience. Dufy's 'Lovely Summer' is all summer in a day, rich with the saturation of happiness. The words in the catalogue seem but a mnemonic of the seed of joy which was buried in the Victorian entrails of South Kensington: 'The countryside in sunshine; in the foreground a river and a fisherman; in the distance cows in a meadow, a cornfield with reapers and harvesters; in the background, the sea with a sailing ship.'

The traditionalism of the themes is as interesting as the digested craftsmanship of the formal conceptions. Brianchon's 'Diana Asleep' is witness of that wedding of France to the classicism of Rome and the Mediterranean of which the first offspring was the school of Fontainebleau. The rabbits in Gromaire's 'Spring' are the lineal descendants of those which nibble the grass around the feet of the 'Dame à la Licorne' whilst Coutaud's 'Orpheus and the Muses' float downstream to the accompaniment of music by some French contemporary of Gluck. There is an abiding sense of the unity of life, of man's ability still to dominate a universe which has done him so great injury,

> 'Terre, Air, Eau, Feu,
> Tapis de mes souffrances,
> Larmes, chansons
> Mon amour et la France.'

There could have been no better comment on Aragon's text than the tapestry of Lurçat.

Saint-Saens and Picart-le-Doux are both artists who have tended to work on a large scale; the one on murals, the other on posters, and both have found in tapestry a way of solving that most pertinent of problems: how to combine large and simple compositions with a sense of fullness and unity. One cannot fill a space six feet square merely by enlarging a smaller creation, and the intense satisfaction to be derived from Picart-le-Doux's 'The Vintage' seems to presage the end of the small easel picture, with its appeal to the individual. The visual arts have their symphonies as well as their chamber music, and tapestry seems to be the heir of the great mural paintings of European art.

The significance of the exhibition far transcended the vindication of the visual genius of France. In an age apt to be dominated by austerity æsthetics and rationed joy it was a compelling statement of the greatness of an inheritance which cannot be traded for a mess of economic pottage. The Minotaur in Saint-Saens' astounding design has at last surrendered to his human foe, and we need not strain our ears to catch its anguished bellowings.

Michael Middleton

FOUR ENGLISH ROMANTICS

THE NEW English romanticism is dangerously fashionable. Critics, breathless from the chase, find in the new movement paper and string with which to tie up week by week in dainty packages the evanescent mysteries of art. Painters who thought, a decade ago, that 'child art' or abstracts were The Thing, now put their signatures to a formula of rugose and ecstatic tree-forms, curdled clouds in lowering skies black with the absorption of light, ripe moons and suns more fiery than that we see through the soft, moisture-laden atmosphere of England. The 'metaphysical assurance' that any group provides in our fractured and ever more complex society, attracts camp-followers as inevitably as a house repaired attracts squatters. But this closeness of group purpose— the result of war-time insularity—though it has been invaluable as a training discipline, is not now without pitfalls. Today, when English painting is more assured than for a century past, we must above all realise that further inbreeding will result only in the self-destruction to which Paris has come. The time has come, I believe, to try and re-assess some trends in the new romanticism.

Why, first of all, the *new* romanticism? If, momentarily and for the sake of convenience, we admit the proposition that with Cézanne an epoch ended, it remains as true of the period since his death as of the period before it, that at all times experiments of a romantic nature have run concurrently with experiments in classicism. Redon, Ensor, Rouault, Chagall, the early Chirico, Klee and intermittently Picasso himself—the threads overlap even if they are not continuous. In this country we have had our subjective painters—Burra, David Jones and Francis Hodgkins, to name but three. Romanticism as such is no more new than ever it was.

It is immediately evident, however, that these artists have been isolated figures; sports, if you like, from the norm. For a hundred years the rising tide of scientific thought has been coaxing European painters into one objective classicism after another. In the flood-waters of the Post-Impressionist revolution, English painting was finally swept off its feet. Perhaps conscious that the logical conclusions and culminations of formal self-sufficiency would prove unhappy garments with which to clothe a love of nature and an essentially lyric view of life, we teetered half-heartedly in the wake of Paris for half a century, fascinated yet afraid, hypnotised by those gay, dare-devil explorers across the Channel. And because we were in strange territory, all our old fears came back, our mistrust of extremes, our reluctance to dedicate ourselves with single-minded passion, our bewilderment and lack of confidence. Strangely enough, it was Paris which gave us a sense of direction again. More than any other single cause it was the surrealist exhibition at the New Burlington Galleries in 1936 which opened our eyes once more to the possibilities of poetic associations in paint and set us free from the pedantic limitations of purely formal values. From about that time date the first cracks in the ice after the long winter. From about that time dates the contemporary English romantic movement as a group activity. To that extent it is new.

What has come to be called the School of London embraces diverse trends. In addition, other developments may be discerned in the provinces, in Scotland and in Ireland. The specific strand which I propose to examine, however, is that which derives from Graham Sutherland, and, beyond him, Paul Nash. For Nash it was, when the geometricism of his middle period flowered under the impact of surrealism into a poetic and mystical apprehension of the *genius loci*, who first succeeded in translating his knowledge into visual terms, and pointed the way to new visual truths.

What is the link that binds the painters forming this particular strand—painters of varying maturity and largely disparate aims? Most obviously, their lowest common denominator is a certain similarity of manner and technique, springing in the first place from Sutherland's own—itself the product of mutual interaction with Moore and Piper. Characteristically, since they are romantics, they seek to exploit to the full the emotional significance of the medium itself. They exhibit a preoccupation with vitality of surface texture and are prepared to combine any combination of media which seems likely to serve their purpose. There has been a great extension of the use of *gouache* (a vehicle which combines fluency with power) harnessed to pen wash and chalk. In oils the approach is frequently not dissimilar, vibration and glow being obtained by a reversion to the traditional method of glazing, often in passages contrasted with opaque pigment and thick *impasto*. The scratched incision replaces the pen line. One recalls the *collage* and *frottage* and realises that the lesson has been learnt. Colour is freed from representational duties and exhausts its emotive potentialities in rich and sonorous harmonies unknown in this country since Turner. And the fact that colour and texture interlock on the decorative plane and exist in their own right is shown more clearly by the re-emergence of the graphic nature of the English genius. These painters do not compose in depth but two-dimensionally. A number, to be sure, find, with Chirico, a ' troubling connection . . . between perspective and metaphysics ' but space is usually represented symbolically; on the surface of their pictures architectonic pattern forms with burgeoning proliferation. This renewed delight in paint as paint, traditionally a French and Mediterranean prerogative, is unusual in this country (though not in Scotland, where ties with the Continent have always been strong). It comes as something of a shock to realise that the sensuous sophistication of our handling of the medium is probably not to be matched anywhere else in the world today, least of all, it seems, in Paris, where the violence of the younger generation's manner prohibits such refinements.

And beyond technique, Sutherland has taught the next generation to penetrate to the very heart and core of things, the most secret innermost places. Nature is not painted on a backcloth but exists around us in full animistic power. As science has pushed the frontiers of physical knowledge inwards to the smallest particles of matter and outwards into space and time, to reach the current paradox that the atom embraces the energy of the universe and is the sun about which our very lives revolve, so the painters have looked further and further, closer and closer, the field of vision has widened and narrowed, until they, too, have reached the understanding that size is meaningless, that the pebble holds within itself the form of the mountain, that the magnification of minutiæ can reveal macrocosmic verities. They apprehend what Baudelaire called the ' universal analogy ' and see, with Blake, the world in a grain of sand. Thorn trees grapple with the sky; lifeless and corroded tree-trunks rear themselves like monsters; mountains burn in the reflection of the fires that created them. Nature is no longer homely, ' sublime ' or merely pretty, a setting for a *fête champêtre*, but cruel and ruthless, sombre and uneasy. It is this intuitive and emotional response which dictates the form of Sutherland's pictures. He does not paint the evidence of a thing, but the thing itself. When other war-artists painted the blitz, they painted—with the exception of Moore—anecdotes more appropriate to the cinema, or the after-effects of something past. Sutherland painted the violence of an actual fact.

This is the single aim common to the younger painters of whom I write. I have referred to them as a group. In fact, there is no group. Half a dozen or so creative painters, moulded in the first instance by innumerable hereditary and environmental stresses and subsequently by chance contacts with traditional and contemporary arts, were influenced for a period by an elder painter. Fundamentally, apart from a common language of manner, they remain separate individuals saying separate things. One may trace a certain progression, from Ayrton on one flank, pre-eminently literary, intellectual and Germanic, through Leonard

Rosoman's visual romanticism and Keith Vaughan's emotional romanticism, to the increasingly formal and classical mode of expression developed by Minton, and further still to, say, a painter like Ceri Richards, whose major work is largely abstract. Each in his own way is seeking to conquer new territory and embrace a wider view of life and man. Sooner or later the artist must face up to the problems posed by man himself. Sutherland has not so far proved conspicuously successful in subduing the human figure to his purposes; Moore has not attempted to relate man to his environment. It is at this point that we really come to grips with the major problem facing the new romantics.

The stable climate of the Mediterranean has produced an extrovert and classical art. Romanticism belongs to the long, dark nights of the north. Nowhere is this shadowy, northern influence more strong than in the work of Michael Ayrton. From Grünewald (and it is not without interest that Sutherland's recent crucifixion for Northampton appears to have been conceived in the shadow of Grünewald), and from the Flemish painters' dæmonic phantasy and bloodcurdling scenes of martyrdom, are derived the distortions of Ayrton's angular, contorted figures, racked with bitter ecstasy. With them he shares an overwhelming interest in mystical experience, and has returned more than once to a subject beloved by Grünewald: the temptation of St. Anthony. Beyond time and space, these symbols of humanity are placed in a cosmos of shifting and dissolving masses of colour, lit by the flicker of candle-flame or the light of his imagination. Dark reds and purples inspire pity and terror. Though the stage-management of his effects is at times a little too theatrically proficient, the best of his religious pictures are conceived with power and passion, and comprise Ayrton's most deeply felt work.

In most of his landscapes the pressures are relaxed. He likes Sutherland's organic tangle and Nash's wide horizon, but he has also been to the potteries and found a sombre beauty among the slag-heaps and the habitations of man. This is important, for today we find romance in the city as well as in nature. Many nineteenth-century artists were fascinated by the novelties of the industrial revolution; more recently Utrillo has looked at the side street and seen more than the flaking plaster wall. But pre-eminently, I think, it has been the cinema which has exploited the urban romantic—the sharp nostalgia of docks, haunted by sirens from far away and long ago; the tensions implicit in the silent doorway; the scutter of paper blowing across the waste plot; the jangle of trams and the rumble of trains over the iron viaduct, and the dank, slime-green mysteries beneath; the wonder of moonlight and the scuttling dog in the hard, hot noonday sun.

Minton has come right into the heart of the city. To be sure, landscape has also provided an outlet for the lyric nature of his vision—perhaps more than any of his contemporaries he has echoed, in his pictures of blackberry-pickers enmeshed in a tangle of matted bushes, indeed in all his landscape drawings, the coruscating proliferation of Palmer, though, inevitably today, with a more tortuous and uneasy note. But he has found, too, in the East End and the riverside, the London equivalent of Berman's Venice. His earlier work on these themes was filled with an intense and tender poignancy; but one or two masterpieces—and I am thinking particularly of his ruined buildings in aerial perspective—could not disguise the fact that the concept was essentially literary. Latterly, he has returned again to the river, but in a far more painterly fashion. Stiffened and reinforced by the example of his contemporary, Colquhoun, and indirectly by Wyndham Lewis, his natural fluency is now forced through a process of formalisation into an ordered, if more impersonal, synthesis, while his palette has broadened to include the strongest colours. The theatrical props and emotive devices of Parisian neo-romanticism have given way to purely visual invention and dislocation of line and tone.

Minton is aware of man, and paints him in relation to nature, to his self-constructed civilisation, to the passing moment, but it is noticeable that in his work man is usually dominated by his background. In Vaughan's work man looms fitfully in the foreground, an oppressed being occupied in some inexplicable activity. Even the most everyday action—one man lighting his cigarette from another's, a workman pushing a barrow—seems saturated with foreboding and melancholy. Faded Georgian façades glimmer in the twilight, a sinister group of outhouses poses an undefined presentiment. One senses, as in the writings of Kafka, the uneasy fabric of a dream. Technically, Vaughan is highly accomplished, though as yet he has not shaken off the mannerisms of Sutherland. His drawing is the result of acute observation and his handling of *gouache* has considerable distinction. If at times he overplays his hand to the point where strength is dangerously near to weakness, it must be remembered that his development has been hindered by army service. He is sure of his aims and of his means, and there appears to be no reason why he should not work a seam of great individuality.

If Vaughan's figures are oppressed by the weight of their own souls, Rosoman's are supremely unconscious of their fate. They are puppets dangling on the strings of eternity, caught unawares by the artist in a revealing moment. Rosoman's acute sensibility and dispassionate observation finds hidden meaning in the visual paradox. His work in the early part of the war, when he was exhibiting with the Firemen Artists, showed a natural vivacity in handling material that was largely illustrative, but its peculiar ' bite ' arose from the slightly mordant and sardonic wit with which he depicted the more bizarre results of the blitz. Subsequently he was commissioned as an official war artist and in that capacity was sent with the navy to the Far East. He speaks himself of the value of this experience. Certain it is that the canvases he brought back showed a remarkable development and a new maturity, though still springing, it seems to me, from the same initial impulses. Two people meeting in a doorway, the one drenched in almost palpable sunlight, the other, inside, cloaked in gloom; the dance of an empty dress in the wind from the tree on which it has been hung; a mountain side bespattered with the little dark figures of Chinese coolies; the mechanistic intricacies of machines of war—from such things does Rosoman construct his pictures with refinement and delicacy. His latest work shows a renewed freedom of technique which promises to lead to a totally unforced and personal manner.

These four painters all see in things a significance beyond the ordinary. Does that represent an escape from reality into a personal dream-world of pseudo-phantasy? I think not. If one detects a certain limitation of mood, it is to be expected. Confronted with the deep malaise of our time, it is the purveyors of the mock heroic, the smug moral and the polite gentility who must defend their work. I think it is arguable that this subjective apprehension of man, opposed in every respect to the academic vulgarities of totalitarian art, foreshadows a return to the humanities. For the best part of a century man has been unimportant to painters except as raw material to be put through the mincing machine of scientific and objective theory. The formalisation and brutalisation of painting in this century has pointed the formalisation and brutalisation of society. A return to the individual and the subjective is a not unwelcome sign.

The real importance of the movement, however, seems to me to lie in the integration of poetic content with more formal values, the fusion of the School of Paris with the English lyric genius. Previously, romantic painters have expressed their feelings about man by filling their canvases with the exotic detail of a distant time and place, by disregarding the constructional demands of their pictures in order that the particular, as opposed to the timeless generality, might gain in intensity. The Parisian neo-romantics and the surrealists, for example, excellent craftsmen though many of them have been, have reacted against rather than profited by the discoveries of this century. Indeed, it was the very completeness of this rejection and independence of formal, plastic values which resulted in the decline or break-up of the groups. When a painter, or a movement, is forced to seek 'subjects' which will suit his theory and technique, rather than expand his theory and technique to embrace the visual wonder of all the world, then the worms of decadence are at work. In their struggle to achieve a synthesis between intellect and emotion, and in their choice of subjects at the very core of life, lies the importance of these English romantics to European painting today.

LEONARD ROSOMAN: *The Quarrel amongst the Sunflowers*

Angry Aeroplanes. Two Avengers on the flight deck of H.M.S. Formidable

LEONARD ROSOMAN

Chinese Junks

The knowledge that they are in fact exploring continents so far un-charted is of inestimable value. Again and again, as Mr. Laurence Gowing has put it, ' it has been the position of English painters to have found discoveries in their hands before they themselves have felt the passion of the search '. All that is changed. We are sensing once again the tingling excitements of the hunt. Free from the burden of revolutionary ideas to which we have not contributed, we are in the main stream again, laying the foundations, it may be, of a new elegiac tradition. As yet it remains a very minor manifestation. Although we have taste, and immense sensibility, we lack power. But since the skies of Europe show no other portents, let us tend the new romantics. Ten years will show and within the next ten years anything may happen.

Michael Ayrton

ENTRANCE TO A WOOD

I DON'T in the least mind admitting that I wouldn't paint trees as I do without having looked at the tree form pictures of Graham Sutherland, at dead trees painted by Paul Nash, at Grünewald's magically distorted trees in the two outer panels of the Isenheim polyptich, at Rembrandt's willows, Altdorfer's pines, Palmer's fat fruit trees, and a host of other pictures. I don't mind admitting further that part of the excitement I experience in painting trees is the result of having looked at pictures of them. I don't mind the influence of all these painters being present in my pictures, in fact I am proud to acknowledge my pictorial parentage; furthermore I am not particularly interested in being ' original.' It may be possible to add an image here and there to the vast vocabulary of images these artists have created over centuries, and that's as much as one can ask, and if it so happens, it comes as a surprise.

Dead tree trunks excite me because of the immobile fury of their arbitrary and abandoned postures. They convey a sense of having died for a lost cause, fighting to the last against an implacable enemy. I am moved by their petrified drama and the frozen anger of their jutting, broken limbs. I would say at once that I am fascinated by this aspect of inanimate objects. I react readily to the dramatic influence of dead and sprawling trees on the landscape about them, but I am as deeply moved by the gamut of emotions living trees can inspire; the genial good-will of trees sunbathing, the terror of bare windblown trees, the lonely grief of isolated trees under rain, or the curious conspiracy of trees in woods.

The Great Yews at Odstock build into caves of dark green that shuts out all but brooding melancholy. They had been at the building of their cathedral for a thousand years or so, but storms and snow broke down their branches so that now they are oppressive caverns through which the spectator moves like a fish in an aquarium. The unchanging foliage of the conifer has a fearful immortality. In high summer, nearby woods contrive a similar impenetrability though their green depths are lush and without the aquamarine hardness of the yew catacombs. On the Wiltshire hills a dense undergrowth is viciously split by the crater of an unrooted birch, a chalk scar surrounded by almost purple earth, and encompassed by root ligaments, which writhe in agony from the wound. The tree is not yet dead. In this way also, the actual Garden of Gethsemane must, I believe, have reacted to the agony of the vigil. The disciples slept through it, but not the trees.

There is something distinctly strange about the behaviour of the trees and indeed of the land in certain parts of Wiltshire and Gloucestershire. It probably appears over-romantic to attribute this strangeness to a mysterious history, but whatever the reason may be, I find the tensity and often anguished vitality of these areas essentially sinister. It was this uncanny sense of pain which provoked my painting of ' Gethsemane ' in Wiltshire, remote though it is from the olives of Judea.

The pictures of which I have written, together with ' Entrance to a Wood,' were all painted in summer. ' The Great Yews ' in July, 1944, ' Gethsemane ' in August of the same year, and ' Entrance to a Wood ' in June, 1945. This latter is one of many attempts to paint the blinding sunlight which presents itself unexpectedly when one comes to the edge of a deep wood. The sudden impact of the hot light on open fields, after the twilight of leaves is to me one of the most exciting of frequent visions. The armed branches and animate foliage, the stark spiked silhouette of the guardian branches leaps and vibrates undefeated by the sun's intrusion. The rooted barrier of the apple tree fights both earth and sun. Entrance and exit are tirelessly challenged.

Trees in winter seem to me to manifest a different kind of power, in which pride, and a kind of impersonal distaste for the bare earth show themselves. There is the same sense in the dead and hollow trunks of unacknowledged defeat and constant battle, but loneliness has taken the place of ferocity. Two pictures I painted in 1945, ' Winter Stream ' and ' Winter Drought,' have no intentional or symbolic connection. They were painted in different years and in different places. Both contain the stumps of willow trees and both are grey with cold save for the smouldering red of brambles and the heat which seems to emanate from bare and distant woods. The willow trunk which rides the bank in ' Winter Stream,' its armour caparisoned with lichen and favoured with ivy, I felt to be a very Quixote, for all its lack of branches a most notable champion. In ' Winter Drought ' the shattered stumps still gesture defiance, though the frosted earth cracks.

The sensation of the unremitting war fought by trees, is one with which I have always experienced. Perhaps it is that I am drawn to paint the more aggressive of the species, for there is much peace to be found in the presence of great elms and oaks. It is I suppose some part of my own nature which is excited by violence and which gives me a greater understanding of the gesticulating apple tree and the twisted willow than the quiet beech or the suave poplar. I imagine that a man paints best that with which he can best identify himself, and if he feels himself struggle he can enter the struggle of his subject. But this is all surmise, and too near the boundary past which words from a painter start to eat into his pictures. What the real process of my painting is I cannot say, nor do I propose to make any rational attempt to find out further, except in the practice of painting. The open secret which I believe is the key to the art, is contained in the word ' identification.'

The act of identification, the painter's passport to the real understanding of form, is much the same as that exercise practised by the Buddhist initiate for the final achievement of ' oneness ' with the divinity. Without this concentrated procedure, even with all the paintings of the great masters to aid one, no true vision of natural phenomena is possible. To paint the essentials of a tree one must come to understand what it is to be a tree, one must become the tree one is painting. There is nothing original in this observation; it is as old and simple as the Book of Genesis, nor within mortal ability does its premise seem easier to fulfil than the acts of creation in that first chapter, except in that one has examples and precedents.

Michael Rothenstein

NOTES AND PICTURES

I. THE SAWN LOG

THE ORIGINS of certain paintings lie buried in a distant past. One day you may decide to paint a tree, a tower, a house; but a hundred earlier impressions have already left their mark. From childhood upwards these have been unconsciously amassed. Impressions, say, of trees; of black clear-twigged elms in winter, of tumbling oaks with russet foliage, of slender trees in spring boiling over with a white fiery froth of blossom. Now each of these impressions has, I think, added its tiny molecule to the matrix in which the present image is so vividly contained.

My subject here was a newly felled redwood pine lying prostrate in a deserted garden. I found it on a winter afternoon. It was growing dark and strips of ragged cloud slipped hurriedly past a screen of poplars and hunched-up pines. The tree was encased in rough scaley bark, mauve-green in colour. Where the trunk had been sawn through, light grain lines made a striking pattern; reproducing in diminishing contours the magnificent outer section. This subject, as I found it in nature, was obscured by a hundred details irrelevant to its essence. A confusion of lopped-off branches, severed limbs whose pink amputations looked queerly human, obscured the more massive elements I sought. . . .

In painting an object the artist is preoccupied with shape and colour. But on the margin of conscious effort other forces are at work. A consciousness, for instance, that my subject suggested the idea of a maimed human corpse played at the edge of my mind. So in painting this picture I was not unaware of these anthropomorphic associations but while at work I thrust them out of sight. For only on the outer circumference of awareness can such feelings exert a legitimate influence. Once pulled from this marginal position and imported more directly as a factor in building one's picture their effect is always detrimental. The overdressed look of much contemporary Romantic painting is due to a too conscious search after subjective drama. The magical, the dramatic elements for which Palmer's art is rightly admired owe their existence to his grip on the tough formalities of pattern. Forms held in sufficient tension generate their own aura of mystery as inevitably as flame produces smoke.

II. 'BRIDGE END, ESSEX'

Whatever the artist is led to find outside himself, by looking, is largely the reflection of something which is already there inside. His physical eye, especially under the stress of strong emotion, can act like the lens of a magic lantern and project outwards into nature, into the forms of clouds and hills and houses, an image which is continually present to his inner view. Even under conditions of only normal tension some such process is at work, persistently guiding and directing the eye to certain curves or volumes which bear a special correspondence with the rhythms pre-existing inside himself. Indeed it is just this reciprocal action—the shapes discovered without giving precision and solidity to the more abstract form-concepts existing within—which produce those memory images which are of the essence of an imaginative vision. It is chiefly this which gives the strong personal flavour to an artist's work, and it is this which would seem to force him back repeatedly to certain typical space relations, a certain type of compositional structure in all his pictures.

Such pre-existent rhythms are the deep-level conditioners—or so one might call them—but of these the artist should remain unconscious. Any insistent probing at these formative levels is likely to interrupt, weaken or even destroy the natural flow of creativeness. But impulses lying nearer the surface may be traced more safely. 'Bridge End' for instance was done during the first phase of my stay in north-east Essex, when, everywhere I went, the magnificent black and white geometry of the farm buildings[1] gave a shock of both surprise and pleasure. I discovered in their abrupt transitions of tone and shape a firm starting point for my own methods of design. At every turn unexpected contrasts held my attention. The triangle of gable-end and dormer, for instance, bluntly opposed the squareness of the house-front—whose livid whiteness was cut by windows (insistently outlined by areas of dark paint), which provided repititions of the rectangular theme. The black skirting too, I noticed, isolated the cottage wall from the rich broken surfaces of ground, just as the blue slate roof, edged with the shadowed guttering, separated it from the sky. An element of conciseness ran all through: a geometric counterpoint curiously exciting in its implications. Other qualities too seemed peculiar to this locality. The village landscape had a knack of paraphrasing its own character and of revealing unexpectedly the basic elements of its design.

[1] The plaster surfaces of these are whitewashed, the weather-boarding tarred.

Plain boxlike cottages of chalky whiteness might be set at angles to each other below the contrasting circle of the winter sun . . . or a lattice of leafless trees might claw the shelving laminations of a distant cloud. . . . Each shape stood out sharp and insistent, shocking the imagination with a dramatic plainness of emphasis.

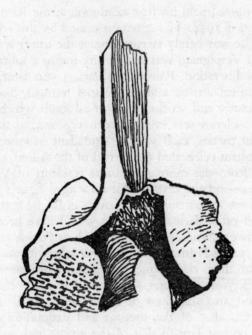

John Fleming

RENZO VESPIGNANI

Renzo Vespignani held his first exhibition at the Roman Gallery *La Margherita* in 1944. The sensation caused by this youth's drawings and paintings (he was barely twenty-one at the time) was all the more startling in that Vespignani was not by any means a solitary talent. For a year after the liberation, Rome, like Paris a year later, was in a state of almost continual artistic and intellectual ferment, and the spate of new books, pictures and works of art of all kinds which cascaded into the shops and galleries was even more overpowering than the galaxy of new political parties, each with its attendant newsheet, with which the ebullient Italians celebrated the arrival of the Allies.

Quite apart from the more permanent residents of Via Margutta—Rome's Chelsea—and the revered but now aged figures of De Chirico and Severini, there were many young artists in Rome at that time whose brilliant though often derivative talents would have been able to hold their own in any exhibition of young English or French artists. Many of them had collected in Rome during the war where it was comparatively easy to conceal their clandestine activities. After the liberation the products of their years in hiding were shown to the public in a series of mixed and one-man exhibitions of great interest and variety, ranging as they did from that of the modish and exquisitely civilised 'surpreraphaelite' Leonor Fini to that of the savage and powerful Renato Guttuso who had seen action with the *Partita Communista Italiana* and whose well-known series of drawings *Gott mit uns* represented the art of the Partisans. But of all these young and vivacious Italians, Renzo Vespignani was immediately and rightly acclaimed as the most promising and original, and he has already had the distinction of being the first Italian since the war to be invited to exhibit in America. As a result, unfortunately, I have not been able to make a very representative selection of his drawings to illustrate this article, since all his most recent and best work has already been sent to the Hugo Galleries in New York.

Vespignani is, of course, a phenomenon. Not only is he master of a fastidious and exquisite delicacy of line (which, I fear, is much coarsened by reproduction) but he was already at the age of twenty-one painting with an assurance that is only attained normally after many years devotion

RENZO VESPIGNANI: *Disegno* (1946),

Vagoni (1946)

RENZO VESPIGNANI

Paessagio dello Scorpione (1946)

RICARDO MARTINEZ :
La Magueyera

MEZA : The Cornfield

DIEGO RIVERA :
*Child Eating
a Torta*

OROZCO :
*The People
of Mexico*
(lithograph)

to the art. It is as a draughtsman, however, that he excels. The richness and variety of the effects that he can obtain with pen and ink are extraordinary; in some drawings the paper is seared with blots and smudges as if by some corrosive acid, in others he employs a calligraphy as sensitive and delicate as the Chinese. One is afraid lest the line will spring up from the paper—it has the nervous tension of a human hair. Though one may, perhaps, discern something childlike in the phantasy which pervades his scenes, there is nothing immature either in the formal conception or execution. In fact the secret of his art may reside precisely in the unnaturally early maturity of his style which has some of the distortions and unhealthy hyper-sensitiveness of a forced growth. Of course, as always with a very precocious artist, outside influences are still very strong though most seem to have been well assimilated. I should mention here, by the way, that Vespignani has never been outside Italy and rarely outside Rome. He studied in a Roman art school for a time, but left it in disgust to work on his own. George Grosz is the most obvious influence and the similarity between his figure drawings and those of Vespignani is too great to be merely accidental. The resemblance is only superficial, however, for Vespignani's essentially Latin instincts and ways of feeling have never been affected by contact with foreign artists and his drawings have therefore none of the brutality of the German's studies of bloated corruption in post-war Berlin. Vespignani is hardly tender and he is not by any means an enthusiastic portrayer of the human animal, but his lines have a spidery elegance and attenuated grace that remind one more of the Decadents and more particularly of Pascin who is, I think, his closest ancestor. Italian influences have been slight though he greatly admires De Pisis; and I suspect he has learnt something from Graham Sutherland, a few of whose war-damage pictures he may have seen at an English Exhibition organised by the British Council in the autumn of 1945. The oildrums in his 'Paesaggio dello Scorpione' are vaguely reminiscent of Sutherland's burnt-out paper rolls. But by whatever perverse combination of influences, he has now created a style both beautiful in itself and perfectly adapted to interpret the subject matter which he has made so peculiarly his own.

But quite apart from the refinements of his style—its curious combination of naïveté and preciosity—Vespignani would be notable as the only Italian artist to derive inspiration from the contemporary scene. Guttuso and others are certainly topical, but their inspiration is less direct, less documentary or *literary* as Italian critics somewhat disparagingly say of Vespignani. Guttuso is without doubt the most important living Italian painter, indeed he is probably the most important young painter in Europe, but he is so precisely because his vision is in this sense purer and the more *literary* elements have therefore been refined away by his remarkable development of the forms of abstract art in the service of his violent Sicilian imagination. Vespignani, on the other hand, appears to have been able to savour with almost Epicurean detachment the grotesque beauties of wartime Italy. He is the painter of the aftermath of war rather than of war itself, and his pictures of the squalid misery and degradation of the war in Italy reflect something of the apathy of contemporary Europe, and evoke that scorching dusty limbo of uncertainty and frustration, the climate of bewilderment and despair that is to be found all over Europe today—in the ruined cities of Germany, in D.P. Camps in almost every country of the continent, in the villages of Jugoslavia and Poland as well as of Italy.

The originality of his interpretation is seen more clearly by comparison with the violence and claustrophobic horror conjured by Moore and Sutherland in their war pictures. His vision is not of desolation and destruction but of squalor and dilapidation, of peeling houses and the drains of life. His *paesaggi* are not scorched and arid but alive—only just alive—and moving with the malignant life of vermin and the putrescent fungi of decay. There is usually a small solitary figure picking its way aimlessly among the debris, overshadowed by a heavy and stagnant-looking sky, and a sodden rubbish-heap or public urinal generally forms the foreground—adequate symbols for the *Zeitgeist*. But even more strangely evocative than these are his drawings of trains. It is odd that so few painters have treated this subject, for trains and railway stations have become for most Europeans an inseparable accompaniment to the miseries of war, only comparable in England with the Tubes and Shelters during the blitz. These trains of Vespignani look rather antiquated and the tracks are but hazily delineated so that they seem to have lost all sense of direction; they have a hopeless and forlorn appearance as if they were being perpetually shunted up some interminable siding. Even for us, for whom trains as such have no special significance, they manage to convey something of the homesickness and baffled exasperation of which they are the symbols for an Italian. They even have something of the inconsequence and nightmare atmosphere of Kafka —a sensation of trying to walk up an escalator that is coming down. As a portrayal of a corrupt world and a tired and effete civilisation these pictures of Vespignani form an astonishing tour de force of disillusion, and will surely rank among the most subtle interpretations of contemporary Europe.

Harold Acton

MODERN PAINTING IN MEXICO

'EXUBERANCE is beauty,' said Blake. And 'the road of excess leads to the palace of wisdom'. Most Mexican painters illustrate these sayings. In Europe we are chary of exuberance and excess; we are suffering from introspective indigestion; we bend the knee to scientists turned art critics; we pay lip service to Cézanne and fail to learn the lesson of Picasso. Our easel paintings are two a penny, but who has the enterprise or stamina to paint frescoes or to promote the painting of them?

One must be prepared to tolerate whiffs of rollicking bad taste, like garlic, from even the best Mexican painters. There comes a sudden climax when bad taste is transmuted into unexpected beauty. This happened in the work of many of the Italian and Spanish *Seicentisti*, with whom the Mexicans offer striking parallels, for they have never quite disintoxicated themselves from their own overpowering Baroque. Very few of them would win approval in the Faubourg Saint Honoré. On the other hand what vigour and imagination, what exuberance and sincerity! These men are free from cramping inhibitions: they may run the whole gamut of political credos but they are painters first, devotees of colour and form, whose brushes and palette are the bread and salt of existence.

It is by their bold experiments in the long neglected field of fresco that the Mexican painters first compel our notice.

My lamented Baroque friend José-Maria Sert was wont to compare easel painting to prose and fresco to verse. For like prose the province of easel painting is boundless, and anything which quickens an impulse to paint may determine the picture which hangs in a room. The fresco resembles verse insofar as it is subject to a discipline imposed by architecture: it must merge into a wall and complete it; it must cling to the wall like skin to human tissue. To understand the requirements of a wall is no easy matter, yet it appears to have been an instinct with the earliest painters, as abstract design is an instinct of primitive peoples. Sensuousness or austerity; a simple or a complicated idiom; fantasy; the relation between crowded and empty spaces—all are imposed, if not dictated, by the elements of the structure.

Originally Mexican painters were drawn to fresco as a medium of popular instruction. As we know from such prehistoric records as the Altamira Cave paintings, it is the most ancient medium of pictorial expression, the earliest manifestation of man's joy in life. José Clemente Orozco, David Alfaro Siqueiros and Diego Rivera were the most clamorous and prolific of the Mexican pioneers, and are usually lumped together in a trio, despite their marked divergences of style and outlook. They were united only in their desire to appeal to the Mexican masses, to teach history, or their own version of it, to the illiterate, to rouse, among other passions, a patriotic pride in their Aztec ancestry. There were extensive walls to be covered in schools and public buildings all over the country, and they covered them from 1921 on.

It takes time to slough the prejudices imposed on one by the mass propaganda of tourist agencies, nowhere more active than in Mexico and always working on the assumption that the tourist is a hopeless loon. Among these is a prejudice against the much advertised Diego Rivera, whose sexy nudes are one of the ' attractions ' of the local Ciro's, perhaps the most extravagant night club in the world. But after seeing a variety of his frescoes in such sympathetic settings as the Cortés Palace at Cuernavaca, for instance, one is bound to relax and enjoy what he has to offer in the way of lush colour and flowing design. Let us not forget Giotto, however. . . . If Rivera is by no means the unique master he is often claimed to be across the Atlantic, he possesses distinct virtues all too rare outside Mexico today. These virtues are racial rather than individual, and Rivera shares them with other Mexican painters to such an extent that, being very prolific, he may be taken as a representative type.

The retrospective exhibition of Orozco's achievement at the Palace of Fine Arts offered a survey of forty years' indefatigable toil. A bewildering cacophony on first acquaintance, it soon resolved itself into an orchestral whole. Even those who disliked it could not shrug their shoulders. There was an avalanche of Balzacian energy in these mural conceptions, of which the first projects and sketches were the finest.

Orozco is a romantic in perpetual revolt. Contradiction is necessary to him. ' Without conflicts,' as he wrote in his autobiography, ' we would have no films or bullfights or journalism or politics or free struggle or anything. Life would be appalling. When anyone says Yes, I have to answer No. Everything should be done against the grain and against the current, and if any fool proposes a solution to smoothe out difficulties it is necessary to squash him, cost what it may, because civilisation itself would be in danger.'

Before he discovered his real vocation Orozco painted grim watercolours of brothel scenes in the full spate of squalid realism, with an evident ' nostalgia for the gutter '. One may admire, with a shudder, the effectiveness of his sprawling unshapely shapes, but there is nothing particularly Mexican about them. They might have been painted by a Frenchman, and the same can be said of Rivera's early canvases, clever pastiches of the French Impressionists, before he developed into a Mexican narrative painter. But Rivera never left the sensuous plane of Gauguin.

The revolutionary movement that began in 1910 with the overthrow of Porfirio Diaz brought home to Mexican artists the wealth of native history and legend at their command, a deep fount untapped since the centuries of Spanish domination. The French School had taught them to observe; now Mexico offered them a wider field of vision. They exhumed the splendours of their buried civilisation and steeped themselves in their indigenous tradition.

Orozco has seldom surpassed his designs for the early frescoes in the National Preparatory School of Mexico City (1922–1926) and his anatomical studies for these, as for his later 'Prometheus' fresco in Pomona College, Los Angeles, show him as one of the supreme draughtsmen of his age. In his early work he could curb his temptation to splash. The tones of his massive 'Cortés and Malintzin', of the Franciscan bowed over a cadaverous Aztec in compassion, of the revolutionary soldiers pursued by their wives with babes slung on their backs—a composition full of heavy, dragging movement—are sober, restrained and appropriately earthy. The figures are austere, discreetly spaced, and free from the chaotic overcrowding of his 'World Catastrophe' fresco in the Palace of Fine Arts and much of his later work. In his preliminary struggle with technical problems he seems to have been disciplined by them. But once the problems were solved to his satisfaction he mounted the galloping steed of *bravura*. There are parallels in music: the soprano running amok with coloratura, the violinist with virtuosity. Starting from caricature he returns to caricature.

The fact that Orozco's major achievement is in fresco prevents him from being well known outside Mexico and the United States. He was born in 1883 in Zapotlán, Jalisco. After graduating from an agricultural college, he studied drawing in the night classes of the Academy of Fine Arts, where the students were made to copy Julien's lithographs. His first impulse to draw came from watching the engraver Posada at work in the window of a painter's shop near his school. Posada was an inexhaustible illustrator of popular stories, ballads and chap-books and has won posthumous fame as 'an interpreter of the sufferings, joys and poignant inspiration of the Mexican people'. He is now considered one of the precursors of contemporary Mexican art. But in the eighteen-nineties the painters most admired, such as Fabrés, imported their paraphernalia from abroad. Cloak and dagger picturesqueness and photographic realism were the order of the day. The Mexican painter still thought of himself as a Colonial, dependent on European standards.

Metropolitan architecture was an inept rehash of French *châteaux* and Swiss chalets; the marble and statuary were shipped from Italy. The Palace of Fine Arts itself is a tawdry Mediterranean product.

Orozco and his fellow students revolted against this blind servility to Europe. Their spokesman, who played a leading rôle in the 'Back to Mexico' movement, was the fiery Doctor Atl, a painter of muscular Titans and volcanoes in eruption, so enamoured of the primitive forces of nature that he made his abode on Popocatépetl. Under his magnetic influence, the younger men realized that they had personalities of their own, 'not pride so much as self-confidence, a consciousness of our own being and our own destiny'. Gradually the Mexican landscape, the forms and colours most familiar to them, glimmered on their canvases like a new dawn.

The decade of confusion following Diaz's dictatorship was a period of storm and stress for artists. A French method of teaching called the Pillet System having been introduced at the Academy, the students went on strike for two years and a few of them, including Siqueiros were arrested for stoning the director. As the revolution followed its course, Carranza, Villa and Obrégon battling against Huerta in the north and Zapata freebooting in the south, and in the subsequent clashes between Villa and Obrégon, when the latter had to evacuate the starving capital, Doctor Atl continued to preach his cultural crusade from the pulpits of derelict churches and launched his paper *The Vanguard* in Orizaba. Orozco and Siqueiros were among its most violent contributors, but after a while they decided that conditions were not favourable to their artistic development. The sufferings of the people, the excesses of the soldiery, the massacres of Zapatistas by Carranzistas, the infinite sub-division of political factions, subterranean intrigues and mutual exter-minations were rather more stimulating from a distance. In 1917 Rivera was in Europe, Orozco went to the United States and Siqueiros followed suit.

By 1922 their prospects at home had improved. José Vasconcelos was organizing a new Department of Public Education and he appealed to all artists and intellectuals to collaborate with him. For a politician to appreciate the rôle of the artist was almost unheard of: had not the great Lord Salisbury maintained that Art is nothing but a trivial amusement of the idle rich? The artists seized their opportunity and those who were abroad rushed back to Mexico. The ground for mural painting had been sown; the ideas which were to infuse life into it had already been churned and formulated. The experience of those who had studied in Europe was useful in co-relating Mexican with modern European art. What differentiated the mural painters from the others was their critical acumen. That this was their historic moment they were happily aware, as of the close relation between their art and modern society. Mural painting broke the routine into which Mexican art had fallen.

Painters and sculptors formed a syndicate with Siqueiros as secretary general, and issued a manifesto to ' the soldiers, workers and intellectuals not serving the bourgeoisie'. Alas, its contents may be guessed: ' Socialize Art. Destroy bourgeois individualism. Repudiate easel-painting and any other form of art sprung from ultra-intellectual and aristocratic cliques,' etc.

To condemn easel-painting is to condemn a major portion of the art of all time, as Orozco realized, and he made some pungent observations about the so-called proletarian art which was the ' legitimate offspring of the syndicate's manifesto '. ' Proletarian art,' he wrote, ' consisted of pictures of toiling workers which were apparently destined for the workers themselves. This was a mistake, since whoever has been toiling for eight hours or so finds no pleasure in being reminded of his labours at home. He will naturally prefer pictures entirely remote from work, something restful to his eye and mind. Proletarian art, however, was purchased at high prices by the bourgeois against whom it was supposed to be aimed, while the proletarians bought the art of the bourgeois, spending hard-earned cash on calendar chromos of privileged maidens lolling on bear-skins or spruce cavaliers wooing countesses on castle terraces in the moonlight. . . . The truth is that good taste is not always innate, or the exclusive patrimony of a determined race or class'.

The manifesto also insisted upon the importance of ' content '—the sum of ideas and emotions expressed in a work of art—which would lead straight back to formless anecdotal painting and the photographic document. To put an end to ' bourgeois individualism ', Siqueiros, upon whom Doctor Atl's mantle had descended, urged groups to work together on a single fresco, each contributing his share according to his talents and following a preconceived plan. The members of the syndicate had decided not to sign their paintings, a resolution which very soon melted away.

The mural painters were chiefly concerned with the history of Mexico and they were passionately pro-Aztec and anti-Conquistador. One is reminded of the Celtic Revival in Ireland: Cortés, like Cromwell, might have lived yesterday. . . . But the Aztec Revival was pictorial rather than literary. Appropriately enough, two of its leading exponents, Juan O'Gorman and Pablo O'Higgins, were of Irish origin. One of O'Gorman's most ambitious frescoes covers the vast wall of the Public Library in Pátzcuaro, Michoacán, and it is crammed from top to bottom with minute historical and legendary anecdotes. A detailed pamphlet has been published explaining the protagonists depicted. These are arranged under forty-seven headings, a compendium more erudite than artistic.

Siqueiros, the most turbulent of the 'big three' and a character of unusual fascination—(Mrs. Trotsky has accused him of murdering her husband)—has dissipated so much energy in revolutionary antics that his achievement falls below his potential. Even so the sheer strength of his work, its momentary power, is undeniable. His pictures bear such titles as 'The Sob', 'Anguish', 'Loneliness', 'Call to Arms', 'Echo of a Scream', 'Sunrise of Mexico'—the latter a squat Aztec woman nursing oil-wells in her capacious lap. But the momentary is seldom permanent, the merely arresting never arrests for long. One wishes that Siqueiros had gone to China to study the strength of the bamboo. In the long sun so much sobbing and gesticulation grow wearisome, and while admiring his Sandow exercises, one suspects that his rhetoric is mechanical. What is this but the 'painting dominated by subject matter' against which he had revolted as a student? I cannot share American enthusiasm for his 'Duco technique'—Duco enamel applied with a spray-gun upon plyboard, the result of which is a harshness of colour repulsively chemical. It is said to last for ever. What of it? Is not the work of, say, Fra Angelico still as fresh as when it was painted?

Fortunately the younger generation have reacted against the dogmatic violence of the older crusaders. Rufino Tamayo and Julio Castellanos are the painters they prefer.

Tamayo is a Zapotec Indian born in Oaxaca in 1899. He too studied at the Academy of San Carlos in Mexico City and rebelled against its rigidity. He has developed a style more consciously aesthetic than that of his peers, more preoccupied with significant form. The colours and designs of his old native pottery seem to blossom again with new meaning in his canvases. His early paintings are purely Oaxacan in theme and colour: a group of Indians standing before their thatched hut like earthenware figures sprung from the soil—there they will remain till Doomsday—or cows grazing in a tropical forest clearing, simplified to the exclusion of all decorative prettiness, deliberately naïf in drawing. As a teacher and director of the Plastic Arts Section in the Ministry of Public Education he made a collection of paintings by children in the primary schools, which appear to have influenced his later trend. He is a living example of the kind of problem that haunted D. H. Lawrence: the young Zapotec Indian going to study in a cosmopolitan metropolis and coming in contact with all sorts of hybrid intellectuals yet forming his judgments apart, travelling, teaching, visiting New York—only to find his way back to his origins, now densely overgrown and entangled in the latest theories and technical discoveries. His forms are ever more primitive, his colours related in harmonies of a subtle crudity, like sensitized stratifications of earth or clay. A sombre archaic dignity distinguishes most of his work, of which photographs can give but a scant idea. As for

Nocturnal Games

CHAVEZ MORADO

In the Plaza

JUAN SORIANO:
The Turtle

RUFINO TOMAYO
The Family

Castellanos, one must suppose that the pronounced static qualities of his Maternities and Nudes exert an exotic charm over the younger painters. Of his work one can always say: ' *Eh bien, c'est solide!* '

Mexican painting seems to have settled down to cultivate its own Hesperides. So effervescing is the wealth of talent that there can be no danger of stagnation. And the diversity of personalities is extreme: Guillermo Meza, José Chavez Morado, Olga Costa, Alfredo Zalce, Raul Anguiano, Ignacio Neféro, Ricardo Martinez, Juan Soriano, each has his own method of cultivating the garden. To offer even a summary appreciation of these painters is beyond my scope.

Guillermo Meza is among the most fertile and protean and he is still under thirty, a self-educated Tlaxcalan Indian, who had a hard struggle before he was able to devote himself to painting. As a child he worked in his father's tailor shop, studied drawing at a night school, earned pittances by retouching photographs and carrying heavy baskets in the market. He drew whenever he had the chance, with any materials he could lay hand on. At times he dreamt of becoming a musician, and music has entered into the texture of his work.

This shy dark boy with the inscrutable mask—he appeared still a boy to my gaze—told me that no composer had stirred him so much as Stravinsky, and, after Stravinsky, Mozart. He has done a series of drawings inspired by ballet, extraordinary records of rhythmic movement in which the nerves and sinews of the human body coagulate into stalactites and crystals; some he has treated like ancient bronzes excavated from volcanic soil, with gaping holes in their flanks, as if to stress that they are but magnificent shells.

In 1938, he showed some of his drawings to Rivera, who recommended him to Ines Amor, and it was this fairy godmother who bought him painting materials and persuaded him to devote himself exclusively to art. Within two years his first exhibition at her *Galeria de Arte Mexicano* enjoyed a sensational success. One cannot foretell in what direction he will develop, for he is always widening his area of observation, and such is his power of receptivity that he will remain in the vanguard of aesthetic adventure. He has graduated from Surrealism with honours. The poetry of earth in him is strong. This is evident in his painting ' The Cornfield ', where a sun-blackened skeleton clad in the white cotton of the Mexican peon stalks between waves of tall corn sloping down from a rocky hill. A twisted tree is hunched behind him, tremulous and dark; the clouds above are billowing in the breeze like the skeleton's clothes. It is a haunting evocation of life and death in the Mexican afternoon, with Nature smilingly indifferent to the *memento mori*, and to the dead animal rotting in an adjacent pool.

A profound melancholy and cosmic voluptuousness are mingled in

Meza's paintings. In some there is a morbid strain—I recall an elemental wolf-boy howling with all his lungs into the wild. Yet as a person Meza is the reverse of morbid, a curious analyst whose first purchase after a successful show of his work was a microscope. He is happy carpentering and dissecting radios, and he is as likely to turn to modelling as to drawing.

What often strikes the foreigner as morbidity is a Mexican idiosyncrasy, a constant awareness of death and an attitude towards it compounded of humour and horror. We find it in bakeries, where skull-shaped cakes are sold for the *Dia de los Muertos*, and at the confectioner's, where sugar skulls compete with cross-bones and skeletons as realistic as they are toothsome. To suck skulls like fruit drops is therefore an experience quite common to most children, and one fraught with festive rather than gloomy associations. The Mexican jokes about death and sends pictures of skeletons to his friends without harbouring any sinister intention. Hundreds of hectic skeletons make merry in Posada's engravings and his series of *Calaveras* are his most characteristic productions.

Other painters very different from Meza introduce skeletons into their pictures with varying frequency. Chavez Morado, who carries on the satiric tradition of Posada in a vigorous style of his own, has painted a dramatic group of soldiers in peaked sombreros shooting at a skeleton. The theme of death is never absent for long. Is not the rock crystal skull in the British Museum the most classical of Mexican carvings?

The vivacious Juan Soriano has done an exquisite picture of a dead little girl laid out on a flowery bier and another of a serio-comic Lyke Wake Dirge. One of Ricardo Martinez's most moving compositions is a ' *Piedad* '—the dolorous mother bowed over the drooping body of her dead son in tenderly eloquent curves. And the solitary ' purist ', Manuel Rodriguez Lozano, an ecstatic painter of dreamlike compositions in moonlight tones, has celebrated death in sixteen panels for Don Francisco Iturbe's home, wherein the horizontal lines symbolize death ' in contrast with the vertical, life '.

Chavez Morado is particularly interesting as a semi-literary *genre* painter-engraver who developed late after a disruptive youth and six years as a roving ' unskilled labourer ' in the United States. Factories and fruit plantations were his academies, his fellow workers were his models, for he continued to draw in spite of his environment. On his return to Mexico the engraver Leopoldo Mendez happened to see his sketches and woodcuts at an open air school, and this chance encounter led to his appointment as professor of the Elementary Arts Department of the Ministry of Public Education. Since then he has spent half his time teaching, but he has also painted frescoes in four public schools and illustrated numerous books with engravings, woodcuts and lithographs.

He did not paint in oils until 1939, when his arduous apprenticeship served him well. He considers himself a realist but he does not think that realism should exclude fantasy. In his opinion fantasy is necessary to give greater emphasis to reality. His landscapes are as quiet and reserved as early Corots. 'People paint Mexico as if it were a blazing Christmas tree,' he remarked. 'The landscape of the central plateau is stark and rugged, its colouring infinitely delicate and evanescent. The cactus itself is a pale, smoky plant.'

Nobody has conveyed more intimately and incisively the peculiar quality of Mexican street scenes, the old tram rumbling along the foolish track beside the Baroque façade, a full moon on a railed-in posturing statue wasting its rhetoric on rows of shuttered windows, a crazy roof-sign in process of construction opposite, the ubiquitous dawdlers, the ice-cream vendor resting lackadaisically against his comic swan-shaped barrow by a white adobe wall while a boy on a contiguous balcony gazes wistfully towards him. There is always more in his pictures than meets the eye. Avoiding the obvious, he captures the *genius loci* every time, and it is not easy to describe precisely how he does it: perhaps it boils down to a subtle selection of essentials. His grotesque allegories are reminiscent of Bosch. Olga Costa, his wife, is a painter of unusual refinement and she shares his ironic humour.

There are others whom I would praise, the recondite Martinez, the architectonic Neféro, and many more. I am convinced that their work would be appreciated in England, where we believe with Blake that ' the world of imagination is the world of eternity '; and it is to be hoped that an exhibition will be organized to acquaint the British public with Mexico's unique achievement in the visual arts.

4

Norman Marshall

A PRODUCER IN SEARCH OF A PLAY

I HAVE been counting up the plays sent me during the last six months.
Nearly three hundred. An average of two a day. Many of them I
returned without reading. The farces, the thrillers and the light comedies.
Some of these may have been excellent plays of their kind, but they
were not of the kind that interests me as a producer. There were other
plays besides these that went back to their authors unread. Plays so long
that they would take four or five hours to perform. Historical plays
in bad blank verse. Plays with impossibly large casts. Stilted, literal
translations of foreign plays. With difficulty I resisted the temptation
to return all plays in which the description of the set mentioned ' French
windows opening onto the lawn '. It will have to be a very good play
indeed which will persuade me yet again to manœuvre a cast for three
acts between the sofa, the easy chair and the bureau which are the
inevitable furnishings of that sort of set.

There were other plays I returned after reading only a few pages,
enough to reveal the fact that the authors were incapable of writing good
stage dialogue. It is astonishing how many people waste their time
writing plays in spite of the fact that they have no gift for writing
speakable dialogue. Stage dialogue is elaborately artificial. It must sound
like ordinary talk, and yet be far more incisive, economical and exact.
It has to be varied for each character in the play. The inexpert playwright usually tries to do this by giving his characters obvious mannerisms
of speech, but in real life differences of speech among people who have
no marked accent is largely a matter of rhythm and length of sentence.
I doubt if any playwright consciously uses different rhythms to char-
acterise his dialogue, but nobody can write good dialogue who has not
got a sensitive ear for the variations of everyday speech and can instinctively use its various rhythms when writing for the stage.

By the time the farces, the thrillers, the light comedies and the plays
obviously not worth reading have all gone back to their authors the
number that remain for serious consideration is not very large. What
sort of play am I hoping to find from among these? The answer is that

I am looking for several different sorts of play. For instance, I am searching for a play by someone who is indignant about something. I don't much care what he is indignant about. His indignation can be moral or political or social or religious. His play can deal with great issues or it can be about some comparatively insignificant episode of everyday life that serves to illustrate the author's indignation against hypocrisy or greed or stupidity or injustice or any of the other weaknesses and cruelties of human nature. Indignation is the theme of at least half the best plays of the 'modern drama' (roughly, the plays written during the past seventy years). It is the subject of most of the plays of Shaw, Ibsen and Galsworthy. It is the inspiration of the crusading spirit that flames in the best plays of Strindberg and Hauptmann. It is what gives edge and bite to the humour of modern satirists as different as the brothers Capek, who satirised over-mechanised civilisation and predatory nationalism, Somerset Maugham, who satirised the standards of 'correct behaviour' in English country houses and vicarages, and Henry Arthur Jones, who satirised the pomposity and snobbery and dishonesty of English society as it was in his day.

Indignation is not, at first sight, the most obvious quality of the work of any of these playwrights. A good playwright knows that an indignant man can as easily become a bore as a man with a grievance. The indignant playwright who is also a good playwright takes care not to shout his indignation at his audience. He expresses it in terms of the theatre, as dramatically and as entertainingly as possible. The most indignant of Shaw's plays, *Major Barbara*, *The Doctor's Dilemma* and *Mrs. Warren's Profession*, are also three of his most entertaining plays, containing some of his funniest scenes.

I find few traces of any emotion as full-blooded as indignation in the plays that are sent me. Often a play arrives on a subject which provides plenty of reason for indignation, but usually—especially if the subject is treated satirically—mere petulance takes the place of indignation. Or the subject is treated with cool, sensible impartiality. The result may be an intelligent, interesting, well-balanced play, but there is no fervour in the writing. In the theatre, indignation and prejudice are far more exciting and effective qualities than coolness and impartiality. One might expect to find the fervour of true indignation in plays with a political theme, but in spite of their noisiness and angriness they are apt to be dry and unpersuasive. A political creed provides poor material for the playwright. It is a ready-made set of opinions which he has accepted because it fits in with his own feelings and convictions. Good plays are about ideas and emotions which the playwright has discovered for himself. There need not be anything particularly new about them. The theatre is not the place for expounding new ideas but for driving home ideas already half-accepted, or for bringing to life again ideas accepted so long ago that they have grown stale and meaningless. That can only be done by young playwrights who have not accepted these ideas but have discovered them for themselves. It does not much matter if what the playwright discovers is already a platitude to most of his audience. Platitudes are fundamental truths which have become worn and dim through long usage. From time to time they need re-stating emotionally and imaginatively so that the audience can rediscover their significance.

What other plays am I looking for? I am searching for an historical play which is not written by an historian turned playwright or by a playwright who has turned to history for a ready-made story as a substitute for his lack of invention. An historical play written because some famous character has aroused the interest and imagination of a playwright, aroused his affection or his admiration or his dislike. If the playwright, as well as painting a portrait with plenty of gusto, has also found parallels in his play between the past and the present, then so much the better. What I do not want are historical plays which reduce great figures to the size of very ordinary people. The playwright can paint his chief character as lecherous, conceited, dishonest, self-seeking, bad-tempered, obstinate, endow him with any characteristics he may or may not find in the history books, but he must not reduce him in stature. The theatre needs outsize figures. In recent years the drama has provided very few, so I have no sympathy with the playwright who goes to history merely to prove that some great figure of the past was just like you or me, or Mum or Dad.

I am searching for a play about one of the fundamental passions of human nature. Jealousy, for instance. A play which does not, like all the plays I have read on the subject recently, treat jealousy as a psychological weakness but as an overmastering, destroying passion. The playwright of today, primed with a little knowledge of psychoanalysis, is more interested in explaining passion that in depicting it. Two of the greatest plays on passion are *Othello* and *The Father*, but Shakespeare does not seek to explain Othello's passion any more than Strindberg seeks to explain the hatred which obsesses the woman in *The Father*. Both playwrights simply show us the appalling effects of jealousy and hatred. In the theatre to watch the havoc wrought by passion is far more moving and exciting than to have the reasons for passion explained to us.

I am searching for a play which takes a group of quite ordinary people and reveals their characters, the whole of their characters, not just those parts of their characters that are useful to the playwright for illustrating a theme and keeping a plot on the move. In fact I am searching for a playwright who can write like Chekov, the first of the realists and still the greatest of the realists. Realism does not consist merely of depicting the more sordid aspects of human nature. That is only a part of realism. Chekov was the complete realist because he told the whole truth about his characters. He passed no judgment on them. Because he was neither a moralist nor a sentimentalist he was not tempted to stress either their virtues or their vices, their strengths or their weaknesses. I have read many plays obviously influenced by Chekov, but their authors in attempting to achieve the tolerance of Chekov have only succeeded in becoming as impersonal as a doctor discussing a patient. Chekov was never aloof from his characters. His tolerance was not of that sort. It was the result of his sympathy for human nature, his understanding, his humour, his gentleness. He saw the absurdities, the weaknesses, the petty little vices of his characters, but he never despised them. He had pity for them, but he was never merely sorry for them. Among English playwrights only Rodney Ackland, Peter Ustinov and a little known author called Anthony Merryn have something of Chekov's ability to see the pathetic weakness of human nature without despising it or passing judgment on it or merely remaining coldly aloof.

I am searching for a melodrama. That, I admit, is a vague and mis-used word. Perhaps it would be better to say I am searching for a Drama. By that I mean a play like *No Room at the Inn*. A great deal of nonsense has been written about this play. Its success has been constantly cited to prove that the public have become interested in plays on social problems. But the public did not flock to the play month after month because they still had any real interest in the sufferings of evacuee children during the war. They went because here was exciting, highly-coloured Drama. The heroine was that unfailingly effective character in the theatre, a real bad lot. There was no attempt to explain her, excuse her or reform her. One was fascinated by her and one hated her. It is good to be able to hate in the theatre. The play was crammed with opportunities for experiencing all sorts of other emotions during the course of the evening. Pity, anger, disgust, excitement. The excitement of the play was partly in the tension created by the situations, but even more in the clash of wills among the lesser characters. Few things are more satisfying in the theatre than a straightforward conflict of character and opinion. The play was full of scenes of this sort. Most playwrights given the theme of *No Room at the Inn* would have treated it much less theatrically. They would have been anxious to be fair to everybody, to analyse and explain. They would not have had the courage to be so frankly and gloriously theatrical.

Dramatic critics often complain that actors tend to underplay because they are morbidly afraid of being ' ham '. Playwrights too seem to suffer from the same fear. Why I, both as a producer and a playgoer, like melodrama is because it gives grand opportunities for all-out acting. It is worth noting that in recent years only two new stars have been ' discovered ' in the London theatre. They are Frieda Jackson and Eileen Herlie. Neither Frieda Jackson when she appeared in *No Room at the Inn* nor Eileen Herlie when she appeared in *The Eagle Has Two Heads* were making by any means their first appearances in London, but it was not until they were cast in melodramas that they found the opportunities to show what they could do.

The greatest weakness of present day play-writing is that it does not make nearly enough use of the actor. The author should regard the actor as his collaborator, not just as his dutiful servant. Managers and producers are often blamed for type casting, but it is the playwrights who are more to blame. Their characters are so neatly and exactly drawn that actors and actresses have to be found whose measurements fit the part in every detail. Good acting parts are roomier than that. They can be fitted to actors of all sorts of different measurements. They demand acting before resemblance. When one is casting Hamlet or Macbeth or Lear one does not begin by wondering whether So-and-So is the right type for the part. One begins by considering whether he can *act* it.

The public go to the theatre primarily to see acting. A passable play with plenty of opportunities for acting has a far greater chance of success than a rather better play in which the cast is asked to do no more than be as unobtrusively real as possible. I have heard many discussions about whether *The Eagle Has Two Heads* ' made ' Miss Herlie, or whether Miss Herlie ' made ' the play. It is symptomatic of the present state of playwriting that there should be such a discussion. There should be no rivalry between actor and playwright. They are collaborators. The good playwright does not try to do the whole job on his own. He leaves part of the work to his collaborator.

In recent years many of our best players have been appearing mainly in revivals. They are unable to find the opportunities for real acting in the plays being written nowadays. The Elizabethan and Restoration playwrights wrote either for actor-managers or for companies in which the shares were owned by five or six of the leading actors. The playwright knew he had little chance of selling his play unless he provided the actors with their opportunities. The playwright of today, no longer striving to satisfy the actor, is content to create good, well-written parts. He does not feel that at all costs, if his play is to be produced, he must give his leading actors at least a few minutes in which they can act for all they are worth. So ' the big scene ' has become a rarity in contemporary drama. In theory it may have been all wrong that the playwright had to pander to the actor to this extent, but in practise I believe it had a thoroughly healthy effect on playwriting. During the next few years the playwrights will have to depend far more on the actors, if only because it is becoming increasingly difficult to find topical subjects for plays. Two wars have destroyed most of the stock subjects of the English drama, the emancipation of women, the conflict between capital and labour, the struggles of the *nouveau riche* to break into society, the tyranny of parents, the woman with a past, the necessity for keeping up appearances, the position of the divorced woman in society, snobbery, social and moral intolerance—all these and many other subjects are finished with forever. There are few new subjects to take their place. In a period as unsettled as the present, the playwright who sets out to be topical may find his subject is already out of date before he has finished his first act.

The playwright must return to the fundamental, unchanging emotions and passions of human nature. To portray them he needs everything that the actor can give him. He must use the actor. He must not be afraid of big, splurgy emotions. He must rid himself of his fear of being vulgar and obvious. The theatre *is* vulgar, in the best sense of the word. It is no place for subtleties, refinements and pastel colours. It should be bold, vivid, garish and exciting. Exciting above all else. The greatest excitement that the theatre can provide is the spectacle of a fine actor in a scene for which the dramatist has called upon him to make the fullest use of his powers. The successful playwrights of the next few years will be those who can write such scenes, write them with a vigour, a sincerity, and an excitement which the actor can match in his performance.

Peter Brook

STYLE IN SHAKESPEARE PRODUCTION

I SOLATION is a very discredited ambition and complete detachment has almost ceased to be a possibility: it is rare for an historian or a philosopher to escape from the influences of his time, and for the worker in the theatre, whose livelihood depends upon his contact with his audiences, this is impossible. Consequently, however hard a producer or a designer may strive to mount a classic with complete objectivity, he can never avoid reflecting a second period—the one in which he works and lives.

In the centuries since Shakespeare's day, the style of presentation of his plays has closely followed social changes. The Shakespeare tradition which exists today is the result not only of the years of scholarship, on the one hand, and of theatrical development on the other: it is the mirror of all the changes in taste that have come about as English society evolved from the uneasy anarchy of Elizabeth's reign to the stable bourgeois pattern of the Victorian era.

Shakespeare's plays were written in a harsh, vital, virile, pioneering age: they grew out of the atmosphere of adventure, of rebirth that came from the final overthrow of mediævalism by the Renaissance. They were conceived in a world of shifting values, of violent belief and violent disbelief, of individualism, ambition, enterprise, imperialism: they were set on a platform stage in the heart of the audience, and their power lay in their closeness, in this ability to play direct on the fantasy by the force of the acting, by the sweep of the rhetoric, and the vividness of the poetry.

When, in the course of time, England became more ordered, politics less open, diplomacy more subtle, and the entire way of living more urbane, the theatre took a gentler place in people's lives. It moved indoors, the seats became more comfortable, a picture frame arose to form a substantial barrier between the actor's emotion and the spectator—and a discreeter public welcomed this protection. In an age of gallantry, the theatre became decorative; the boy was replaced by the actress; the O of the imagination by the painted cloth; and the uncouth edges of passion softened by the charms of incidental music. When Garrick played Romeo in wig and knee-breeches, the play became eighteenth century, and the Juliet a Beauty of Bath.

From Garrick to Kean, from Macready to Irving, production style was moulded by social history. As the melodrama houses became popular, as the music halls opened their doors, the groundlings ceased to patronise Shakespeare, and with them some of the fibre went out of his plays. The violence was diminished, the bloodshed reduced, the frankness of language veiled to spare the ears of the new middle-class audience on whom the box-office was coming increasingly to depend. The importance also of the upper classes had diminished: the days were gone since they were the patrons and could call the tune and the aristocratic part of Shakespeare's work—the skilful word-play and the learned pun—became dead-wood. The texts grew shorter, the scenery more opulent. The tragedies of Shakespeare had become shows, ideal for family outings, inseparable companions of the souvenir programme and the chocolate box.

Shakespeare production today is based on a number of axioms whose presence no one even troubles to question. It seems inevitable that the plays should be divided up into acts and scenes, it seems inevitable that the *Midsummer Night's Dream* should have gauzes, ballets and Mendelssohn, that Romeo and Juliet should be middle-aged, that the histories should be played in front of tapestry curtains—red for England, blue for France: it seems inevitable that one should have to change pieces of canvas to indicate to the audience the difference between the outside and the inside of a castle. Yet few people wonder, in fact, few people are aware that the stage directions in their editions of the plays, the eternal 'Another part of the battlements', 'A forest', were all inserted by eighteenth-century editors. Few people give sufficient consideration to the fundamental difference between a play conceived as one whole poem, written in verse and designed to be played with the sweep and the freedom of verse, and one that is continually broken in line, and converted into a row of static units by the sequence of irrelevantly localising scenery. This realistic scenery has led into a vicious circle. The more elaborate it becomes, the more the sequence of the play has to be broken, and the more the play has to be cut down. It has led to the immense barrier between play and audience that a cliché devotion to period accuracy has created. Poetry is sacrificed to pedantry, and in the meaningless search for historical accuracy, inner reality is smothered by fancy dress.

The greatest mutilation which Shakespeare's plays have suffered is in the attitude of the actors. Through centuries in which actors have been their own managers and producers, the emphasis has not been on plays but on parts. The star actor has cut down all the supporting scenes with their richness of character and background detail, has given smaller parts to indifferent actors and pushed them into insignificant positions. In doing so, he has completely destroyed the balance of the plays, for to

Shakespeare each character was of equal importance, and whosoever happened to be speaking at any given moment was for that moment the 'lead'.

This is the main tradition in Shakespeare production today, and is the tradition to which so many of our scholars and critics have become completely accustomed. It is only by close study of the plays, that one appreciates the astonishing gap between one's preconceptions and the actual text. One discovers how the direct line of tradition from Elizabethan to Victorian has now reached a full stop, and how a century which has, socially, swung back to an atmosphere closer to that of Elizabeth's England than at any point in the last four hundred years, must find a new style and a fresh approach.

One of the greatest possible errors that a producer can make is to believe that a script can speak for itself. No play can speak for itself. If an actor delivers his lines clearly but monotonously, no one will think that he is doing his job well. However, it is still widely believed in this country that the flat and static production is good, whilst the one that uses all the resources of theatre to illuminate the text is said to obscure the play. Indeed, in England, far too large a proportion of intelligent playgoers know their Shakespeare too well. They are no longer capable of going to the theatre with that willingness to suspend disbelief which any naïve spectator can bring. They go coldly, as specialists, to listen to the over-familiar lines, and to watch the actor's treatment of them. It is their influence on the theatre that has led to the type of Shakespeare production that is not uncommon nowadays, cold, correct, literary, untheatrical, winning great praise, but making no emotional impact on the average spectator.

The school of Poel and Granville-Barker rendered a great service to the theatre by its reaction from the excessive elaboration of the His Majesty's style of presentation. However, it went to the other extreme and sought simplicity in retrogression. It believed that the panacea was to go back to the conditions of Shakespeare's day and perform his plays on an Elizabethan stage. It is impossible truly to re-create this inside a modern theatre. To be consistent, one would have to re-create the entire Elizabethan theatre, with its crowd, its noises and its smells. Even supposing one were to achieve a complete reconstruction, one would find that the spirit of Shakespeare had once more slipped away, and that in one's search for the lost Shakespeare one would merely have created a Shakespeare museum.

It is a grotesque over-simplification of the problem to believe that anything can be achieved by going back on the developments of the theatre in the course of the last few hundred years. It is as incongruous as to suggest that the cinema should become silent again, or that classical music should be played on the primitive wind instruments of Mozart's day. Realising this, a number of producers attempt a compromise. Within the pictorial conventions of the present day proscenium, they build a structure that fulfils the necessary geographical qualifications of the Elizabethan stage, and yet can be used and lit as though part of a modern production.

This method falls dangerously between two stools. It aims at freeing the text by turning the set into a formal platform, but it fails to recognise that simply by being inside a proscenium it ceases to be a platform and becomes a picture. The Elizabethan stage was completely undistracting because it was out-of-doors, because it was merely a rostrum jutting out like a pier among the spectators. Its structure was something quite irrelevant, and consequently quite invisible, much as the grey-coated stagemanagers who flit to and fro across the stage in a Chinese theatre are completely unnoticed by the audience.

However, no sooner is this same Elizabethan theatre, beam for beam and inch for inch, placed on a modern stage, than it becomes a picture; it ceases to be formal, it suddenly asserts its period, and when the producer still further compromises by using realistic lighting effects, the breakdown of style is complete. The error is very similar in modern-dress productions of Shakespeare. They emanate from the theory that modern clothes, like the contemporary clothes which the Elizabethan actors wore, are completely functional, and thus the least distracting form of costume for a tragedy. However, the Elizabethan actor was playing in his modern clothes on his formal platform stage; actors inside a picture frame are always actors in a period costume, even when the period happens to be the present day. One can not escape from their incongruity, and in the last resort they are less functional and more distracting than the most ornate of dresses.

When an audience enters a theatre, its imagination is completely open. If, as in *Our Town* it finds the curtain up, the stage bare, then the initial anti-pictorial gesture of the production makes it clear that no picture is going to be presented, and that the proscenium is merely an arch over a square of boards on which the actors will seek to create an illusion. Thus in the opening gambit the conventions are established, and the audience's imagination is liberated, leaving it both ready and capable of creating its own pictures. However, if the curtain is lowered, if, when the lights fade and the curtain rises, one sees a structure with period decoration, if the lighting suggests even as elementary an atmosphere as day or night, already the audience has accepted a pictorial convention, and at once surrenders its imagination into the hands of the producer. This imposes a heavy obligation on him not to betray his trust, and if he tries to compromise by allowing the play to be semi-formalised, instead of going all the way pictorially, the audience will feel cheated. It will neither have the satisfaction of exercising its own imagination, nor will it have the thrill of yielding to a continually imaginative and convincing stage illusion. The great percentage of Shakespeare productions that one sees today are dull simply because they make this compromise: sometimes through fear, sometimes through modesty, sometimes through lack of ability the producer fails to fulfil the tacit offer which he has made to the audience.

Musset says that a door must be either open or closed, and we can say with equal simplicity that a production cannot toy with illusion—it must either go all the way or none of it. Both are legitimate, and both can be achieved, but neither can be found by retrogression. It is possible to achieve on the present day stage the formality of the Elizabethan, but only by totally different means. Above all, the means employed must be self-consistent: if the pictorial convention is to be rejected then the curtain must not be used, the lighting and the decorations must at no point suggest whither time or place, period or atmosphere, the stage structure must be made a platform to which they serve the neutral purpose of background and illumination. Similarly, the costumes must be clearly uniforms for actors, satisfying the eye but suggesting neither the past nor the present. Such a technique, like that of the Chinese or Japanese theatre, would make the plays rely exclusively upon the words and the actors, and potentially could give the purest and most æsthetically satisfying renderings of Shakespeare's plays.

Practically speaking, this approach has two great dangers. One is that by placing such complete emphasis on the actor it also imposes upon him a burden that very few casts would be qualified to bear. A large part of the work of every producer is to find external means of supplementing the work of the actor when this cannot rise to the expressive requirements of the moment. If the actor is left on a bare stage with nothing to create a mood for him, and nothing to help him, he must be capable of holding the full attention of the audience every instant by himself. With an ideal company, such a production of Shakespeare could be envisaged. Even then, one would have to take into account the reaction of the audience. The theatre, unlike any other art, is empirical. It has no existence until it exists in front of a spectator, and beyond a certain point it cannot lead further than an audience is prepared to follow. A naked and simplified production of Shakespeare might have great virtue, but it would be of no practical value if it proved to be too rarefied and austere in its idiom for the average person.

Shakespeare is the world's most popular dramatist: his plays have been more played, more translated and more read than those of any other writer. When it then appears that in his own country in the twentieth

century he has become one of the least-performed dramatists, it is clear
that the method of presentation is at fault. It also follows that popular
success must be a very considerable criterion for a Shakespeare production—a production that succeeds is not necessarily good, but one that
fails where the appeal of the play has long been established must undoubtedly be on the wrong track.

To communicate any one of Shakespeare's plays to a present day
audience, the producer must be prepared to set every resource of modern
theatre at the disposal of his text. This text will be obscured by a mass
of false traditions, by archaisms, by meaningless references, by out-moded
conventions, by the thousand technical differences that the different
theatre building of Shakespeare's day dictated. The producer must be
able to discriminate between these externals and the essential living heart
of the play—the poet's inner dream—for which it is his job to find
theatrical correlatives.

In my own production of *Love's Labour Lost* the play was dressed after
Watteau—a period 150 years after the play was written. This choice of
costume was not dictated by any *a priori* considerations, and historical
accuracy was rejected as of supremely little importance. I chose Watteau
because the style of his dresses, with its broad, undecorated expanses of
billowing satin seemed the ideal visual correlative of the essential sweet-sad
mood of this play. In the scenes of the Princess' court, I introduced a
chalk-faced, white-clothed zany—a character in no way suggested by any
line of the script but who remained to the end as a forlorn, drooping
symbol, in period as much Schumann as Shakespeare, of the atmosphere
of these scenes. In the more sturdy comedy scenes Dull, the constable,
had the bright blue uniform, the eternal truncheon, helmet and string of
sausages that symbolises all policemen—Toy Town, Victorian London,
Harlequinade or Navarre—and helped to communicate in one glance to
the audience the image that springs to mind the moment one reads his
name. The congruities and seeming incongruities of this production
were all dictated by the expressive requirements of the script, and my
claim is that through this fundamental consistency they were bound
by one style and acquired their own truth. As innovations, they
scandalised the specialists but pleased the public, and when the production was revived a year later they had, it seemed to me, been completely
accepted.

In *Romeo and Juliet* the problem was above all to find a modern stage-
craft which could give freedom and space to the sweep of the poem.
The time for the assumption that *Romeo and Juliet* is a sentimental story
to be played against a series of backdrops giving picture-postcard views
of Italy must surely be gone. It is a play of youth, of freshness, of open
air, in which the sky—the great tent of Mediterranean blue—hangs over

LOVE'S LABOUR'S LOST
Stratford-on-Avon
(production by Peter Brook)

[*Angus McBean*

PETER BROOK rehearsing
Love's Labour's Lost

LOVE'S LABOUR'S LOST,
at Stratford-on-Avon
(production by Peter Brook)

ROMEO AND JULIET at Stratford-on-Avon (production by Peter Brook)

DAPHNE SLATER as Juliet in *Romeo and Juliet* at Stratford-on-Avon (production by Peter Brook)

ROBERT HELPMANN in
Apparitions, choreography by
Frederick Ashton :
Sadler's Wells Ballet

[*Cecil Beaton*

MARDI GRAS, choreography by Andrée Howard and Hugh Stevenson : *Sadler's Wells Ballet*

LA FÊTE ÉTRANGE, 1947, choreography by Andrée Howard : *Sadler's Wells Ballet*

MARGOT FONTEYN and ALEXIS RASSINE in *Giselle*, Act I, at Covent Garden

[*Baron*

MARGOT FONTEYN and ALEXIS RASSINE in *Giselle*, Act II, at Covent Garden

[*Baron*

PILLAR OF FIRE, choreography by Anthony Tudor : *Ballet Theatre, New York*

LA FIANCÉE DU DIABLE, choreography by Roland Petit : *Ballet des Champs Elysées*

every moment of it, from the first brawl in the dusty market to the calm and peaceful cadence in the grave. It is a play of wide spaces, in which all scenery and decoration easily become an irrelevance, in which one tree on a bare stage can suggest the loneliness of a place of exile, one wall, as in Giotto, an entire house. Its atmosphere is described in a single line, ' these hot days is the mad blood stirring ', and its treatment must be to capture the violent passion of two children lost amongst the Southern fury of the warring houses. Any approach to the play that takes as its starting-point its essentially virile and very Elizabethan spirit soon finds that there is no place for sweetness and sentimentality in the characterisation, in the speaking, in the settings or in the music. I endeavoured to make the Stratford *Romeo and Juliet* essentially 1947 in its approach to the staging, and essentially Elizabethan in atmosphere, and I believe that, in practice, it seemed both true and alive to the theatre-goer who had not over-close acquaintance with the play.

Unlike any other artist, the theatre producer must be continually aware of his audience. He must work to communicate to a specific mass of people, and their immediate reaction is his only measure of success. A production of *The Tempest* that might be good in Moscow could just as well be bad in London, much as the way of interpreting the same play to Norwegians should differ radically from the manner of interpreting it to Latin Americans. The production of *Romeo and Juliet* in Prague which set it in a concentration camp might well seem preposterous outside Czecho-slovakia, but in that country at the instant at which it was produced it had a peculiar meaning and poignancy that was the cause of its great success.

The producer is working with three elements: his text, his audience, and his medium, and of these only the first is constant. It is his primary duty to discover every intention of the author and to transmit these with every possible means at his disposal. As the theatre develops, as its shape and geography, its machinery and its conventions change, so production style must change with it. There is no perfect production of any play, nor is there any final one: like a musician's interpretation, its existence is inseparable from its performance. A production is only right at a given moment, and anything that it asserts dogmatically today may well be wrong fifty years from now. The theatre deals with living material and is in an endless state of flux. When a new actor enters a company the treatment of his scenes should be amended; if a play is revived, changes must be made. Any attempt to fix productions by tradition is doomed to lead to the lifeless cul-de-sac of National Theatres.

When Garrick played *Romeo and Juliet* in knee-breeches, he was *right*; when Kean staged *The Winter's Tale* with a hundred Persian pot-carriers, he was *right*; when Tree staged Shakespeare with all the resources of the His Majesty's, he was *right*; when Craig staged his reaction to this he was *right* too. Each was justified in its own time; each would be outrageous out of it. A production is only correct at the moment of its correctness, and only good at the moment of its success. In its beginning is its beginning, and in its end is its end.

Norman Nicholson

THE POET NEEDS AN AUDIENCE

THE POET needs an audience. This is not just for his encouragement, but because to be itself poetry needs to be heard even as music does. The score is only the bones of the symphony which does not exist as such until it is fleshed in sound, and poetry on paper bears the same relation to the true poem as does a photographic reproduction to the original painting. On paper the reader can study the shape and substance of the verse, but it does not become a poem till it is alive at his lips or, at least, at his ears. But the poet today writes for a people most of whom have never learned to read. Instead of reading they glance over, and they have developed a sort of visual Braille, by which they recognise the shapes of letters and groups of letters and even of whole phrases and blocks of type without really translating them into words at all.

Now this method, which is admirable for the quick gathering of information, is quite useless for reading poetry, yet for the majority, it is the only method they know. They skim through a poem as if they were searching for a name in a telephone directory, and then wonder why they have not understood. This sort of visual reading is probably a fairly modern development. The people of ancient Greece and Rome seem to have read at the speed of speech, and even to have ' mouthed ' the words as they read, and the leisured classes of the seventeenth and eighteenth centuries must have learnt the art of slow and careful reading by study. But today though a poet may have his work printed in a miscellany which reaches tens of thousands he cannot be sure that more than a handful will really *read* it. It has got somehow to catch not just the public eye but the public ear.

There is, I believe, a large potential audience among those who as yet have not responded to poetry merely because they think it should be seen and not heard. They do not like poetry, not because they are incapable of appreciating it, but merely because they do not know what it is. If the poet can speak to this public through the stage or through radio, he may find that he has a larger audience, and, what is more important, a more varied audience, less specialised, less restricted to those of one class or section of society.

In the theatre the audience itself contributes to the performance; there is a flow of sympathy between actor and spectator so that the latter helps to create the scene which he sees. This act of co-operation is one for which the present-day poet should be particularly grateful, for he is finding himself more and more isolated from his fellows by the very nature of his calling. In other aspects he is in fairly close contact with them, for he rarely belongs to a leisured class and the tradition of Bohemianism seems to be on the wane. Moreover, he has to earn his keep and to live a more-or-less ordinary sort of life—all of which is likely to be to the good. But *in so far as he is a poet* he tends to be severely separated even from those of whom he sees most.

It is in the theatre that the poet can find sympathy and response which otherwise he must get from his readers, who (unless he lives in London or some similar centre) are scattered as thinly as neighbours in the Arctic Circle. In the theatre, however, he will find an audience not restricted to his readers, an audience varying greatly in its powers of appreciation and understanding, but one which is yet more complete and more satisfying than the most perceptive individual reader. The Elizabethans wrote for a very mixed crowd, from the groundlings to the aristocrats, and Shaw would have us believe that the need to please everybody was irksome and restricting, and that Shakespeare contemptuously added slapstick and romantic comedy when he would have preferred to get on to his high tragedy. In truth, the plays gained immensely in virility by the fact that they were written by a whole man for a whole audience, and we cannot believe that Shakespeare would ever have been Shakespeare if he had been restricted to the writing of masques for the Court. His genius would certainly have found some means of expression, but I do not think it could have developed fully had it not had the stimulus and response of an audience as lively and mixed as that at a street procession, as curious and critical as that at a Lancashire League cricket match. Prospero needed both Ariel and Caliban.

My point is that those who were unable to appreciate the poetry and the subtlety of Shakespeare, would nevertheless be able to enjoy the plays after their own fashion and in doing so they made a real and necessary contribution. Without that contribution, the Elizabethan drama would have lost much of its vitality and have become a partial thing. In the same way, if the modern poetic drama addresses itself solely to that public which reads poetry, then it will become weak and etiolated and will never develop into the drama which the theatre so badly needs. This does not mean that the poet must write down to his audience, but he must be prepared, obviously, to make his words intelligible *at the speed at which the listener receives them,* and he must provide enough of action, plot and character to keep the whole of the audience entertained and interested even if the deeper significance of his symbolism is missed by some of them, even, perhaps, by most. He is not obliged to write for nitwits, but he should have a reasonable respect for the man who, without special knowledge of modern poetry, is ready to pay his half-crown and listen honestly and attentively. That man is an essential part of any normal audience. To ignore him is to leave a hole in the picture, but once his curiosity is roused and held, he does not object if the poet piles up fantasy and symbol, indeed he may enjoy and understand him better than he himself knows. A play is a public poem, orchestral in form, and it will be very thin music if the bass and the brass are left out.

Those modern poetic plays which have been widely successful seem to me to have achieved their success because, like Shakespeare, they appealed simultaneously at various levels of perception. *Murder in the Cathedral,* for instance, has been performed all up and down the country, in villages and camps as well as in towns and cities. Only a small number of the audiences which saw it can have appreciated to the full Mr. Eliot's study of the nature of sainthood, of the complete subjection of human will to the divine will. They saw it, instead, as the story of a man ready to die for his conscience, a martyr for the freedom of belief, a thoroughly English and Protestant hero standing up for his rights against authority. In the same way, many of those who saw *The Ascent of F6* must have been puzzled by the Freudian and political symbolism, but their interest was held by the fairly straightforward story of the attempt to climb the mountain. Moreover, I do not think the poet need be discouraged if the full significance of his play is not at once evident to his audience. To my mind, symbolic meaning (as distinct from allegoric meaning) can often be perceived and understood by the reader or listener without his being aware even that there is a symbolic meaning. *The Pilgrim's Progress,* for instance, has its obvious allegorical message made plain for everyone by the names of the characters, but, at a deeper level, perhaps undesigned by Bunyan himself, is the splendid symbol of the struggle and the journey, which belongs to the world of myth and epic. Throughout the nineteenth century *The Pilgrim's Progress* was the second Bible of the nonconformists. They learnt it by heart, preached on it, and some of them lived by it. It was, of course, only the plain allegory with which they were concerned, and they never even suspected the deeper symbol, yet I am certain that in their imagination they recognised and responded to the full poetry and implications of the book.

The poet in the theatre of today, however, must not merely adapt himself to his audience, he must create an audience to which to adapt himself, for the tradition of the poetic drama has died out in England so far as theatre-going is concerned. The poet, therefore, is almost bound to address himself to those who do not particularly want to hear him. Both the plays I have mentioned were intended primarily for a particular group: *Murder in the Cathedral* for the Anglicans, and *The Ascent of F6* for the Left-Wing, and both by this means were able to appeal to a much larger public than that which had read *Ash Wednesday* or *The Orators*. I think that, at the time, this was tactically wise, and it was certainly successful, but while the method of writing to a prescribed audience may be justified theatrically, it is obviously unsatisfactory to the poet himself. He feels that his work is being praised or criticised for the wrong reasons, and that much of his poetry is being misconstrued to fit the preconceptions of others. Auden's third play, *On the Frontier*, seems to me to have a certain sterility due precisely to this, and Eliot, seeing the danger, has made no attempt to repeat the same sort of success as that of *Murder in the Cathedral*.

When the modern poetic drama began to emerge in the works of these playwrights and also of Yeats, it disclaimed—rather too self-consciously, I think—all connection with the show next door, the 'realist' prose drama of Shaw, Galsworthy and the rest. About ten years ago Mr. Eliot gave a radio talk to schools in which he said—if I remember him rightly— that it was necessary to emphasise that the poetic drama was different from the prose drama not only in manner but in kind, and also to remind the audience of this difference by the use of rhyme, song, chorus, or other stylised techniques. Now I am doubtful whether it is true that the poetic drama is different in kind from prose drama, or not, at any rate, from the true prose drama of Congreve, Goldsmith, Wilde and Shaw—that which we commonly meet in the theatre today being a debased product. Nevertheless, the return to a stylised drama, the return to artifice (whether it be the artifice of the liturgy or of the music hall), the reminder that the drama had its roots in ritual—all these have been of great value, have produced the finest poetic drama of our century, and will probably continue to do so. In spite of this, I feel that the time is now past when poetry should dissociate itself entirely from the 'realist' drama, and while experiment and discovery go on, let poets see if it is not possible to reconcile the aim of the poet with the needs of the popular theatre.

The great revival which started in the 'nineties has now run down, but the 'realist' theatre has still much to offer. First of all it has an audience, less devoted, less enthusiastic, perhaps, than it was thirty or forty years ago, but with a tradition of loyalty, of curiosity and of seriousness. A mixed audience, a popular audience (in the sense that it cares nothing for fashions and is ready to do without comfort), and, above all, an audience which is not exclusively metropolitan. The great repertory movement of the early part of this century not only diffused the influence of Shaw and the others throughout the country, but encouraged the growth of regional drama, and so strengthened itself and enriched our culture. This audience, I think, still exists—it certainly does in the provinces—and though now it has to live mostly on revivals or on second-rate products of the last fifteen or twenty years, it is still adventurous and eager.

The second and, more important, offering of the 'realist' drama is its convention, which I would define loosely as the convention of the empty fourth wall—of the audience as spectators, and of reasonably realistic dialogue, action and portrayal of character. (I say *reasonably* realistic because it should include plays like *St. Joan*, *Androcles and the Lion* and *Tobias and the Angel*, where, obviously, photographic realism is never intended.) When realism becomes mere photography and mere reporting it turns the theatre into a second-hand clothes shop. When it is patched and partial, allowing false value and sentiment but insisting that every sleeve shall be the right length and that every mouth shall be denied all but the shoddiest words, then it is not only dull but dangerous. The poets were certainly right to revolt against this, but was it necessary to try to destroy the illusion of the picture-frame stage altogether by bringing in actors from the back of the auditorium, by backchat between the actors and members of the audience, and so on? Too often these have the effect not of breaking the convention, but of emphasising its occasional awkwardness. When the audience has booked seats, chatted in the foyer, bought programmes and settled down in tip-up chairs, it is far too conscious of the theatre to be persuaded by a few tricks that it is really in a church, or a market-place.

However, I do not want to criticise the stylised drama but to point out that the audience is used to the convention of the picture-frame stage and of a fairly reasonable imitation of the appearance of life. Given this it is at home, it is ready to be receptive, and its first line of resistance is broken down.

If the poet decided to speak to this audience in a convention which is not too unfamiliar he still has two great problems to solve, that of form and that of language. Of the problem of form I will not speak—it is scarcely even beginning to be solved. Looking round at the modern poetic drama, I cannot guess which way it is likely to develop, and while it is obvious that the very possibility of a poetic drama in the future depends on its finding a form, yet I think that the poets themselves are more likely to be concerned first of all with the problem of language. Dramatic critics are apt to complain of poets that their plays are not well-made, not as effective as, say, an Aldwych farce, but I feel that they scarcely realise the enormous difficulties which face a modern poet on the stage today. He has no accepted form or standard to follow, and he has no convention of language. Could you, for instance, ask for a boiled egg in verse?

Mr. Ivor Brown and other critics would point out that the Elizabethans could, and would advise us to return to blank verse. But dramatic blank verse was already beginning to disintegrate before the end of the reign of James I, and today it drags with it the dead weight of all those unacted and mostly unactable plays of the nineteenth century. To write blank verse for the stage seems to me to accept from the start that your play will be read rather than acted, in spite of the example of Mr. Peter Yates, who used iambics in *The Assassin*, the most interesting attempt yet made by a modern poet on the realist-biographical type of play. Mr. Montagu Slater argues that a 4-foot, not a 5-foot line, is natural to modern speech. Mrs. Anne Ridler may agree with him, for she uses a 4-foot line in *The Shadow Factory*, though in *Henry Bly*, a new, as yet unpublished play, she has found it necessary to broaden the line frequently to five stresses. Mr. Slater's opinion particularly interests me, for we were near neighbours in boyhood, and therefore share the same native idiom and accent, but while the 4-stress line was certainly effective in the sung dialogue of *Peter Grimes*, it is, I feel, too jerky for sustained speech. Mr. Eliot, in *The Family Reunion*, fashioned a form of verse in which he could pass from trivial conversation to the heightened speech of incantation without any incongruity or change of gear, but his example, magnificent as it is, is not as yet defined clearly enough to be a general model. Some poets, including Mr. Ronald Duncan in *This Way to the Tomb*, vary the form of verse to suit the occasion, a method which is attractive and may be effective, but is certainly risky. Others quite frankly lapse into prose. This is what I have done myself, and I do not think it is necessarily an admission of failure. The blending of prose and verse has fine precedents, and it need not disturb the unity of the play if both poetry and prose have a common diction and idiom.

This leads me to perhaps the most vital problem of all—that of diction. During the last twenty or thirty years there has been a revolution in poetic diction as drastic as that made by Wordsworth. The diction of the nineteenth century has been decarbonised, and a new vocabulary made available, but I do not think that poetry has anywhere really touched common speech in the way that it did in Wordsworth. Once a true relationship has been established between poetry and contemporary speech then it is possible to heighten and embellish that speech both in diction and rhythm without losing its essential naturalness. Thus the Elizabethans were able to build up a magnificent façade of words because underneath was the plain, homely stone:

> ' It was a lover and his lass
> That o'er the green cornfields did pass
> In Springtime,'

And Ford could take simple words and lay them side by side like pieces of coloured glass for the light to shine through them:

> ' *Fernando, in short words, howe'er my tongue*
> *Did often chide thy love, each word thou spak'st*
> *Was music to my ear; was never poor,*
> *Poor wretched woman lived that loved like me,*
> *So truly, so unfeignedly.*'

It is true that the form of common speech which has so far been accessible on the modern stage has been that of suburban English, and this is certainly not very hopeful material for poetry. It is an oddly DIS-LOCATED speech, its vowels distorted and curled into tripthongs, like the needless windings of its roads, and its natural idiom dug up, carted away, and replaced by concrete paths and wooden gates and whatever mass-produced ornaments are handy. It belongs neither to the country nor to the town. It is so badly tended that when an aerodrome or a factory moves near it, slang grows over it like weeds in a few months. The rowan of the fellside is there, tamed to a wrist-thick sapling which each year produces a few berries for a home-made sauce; the turf of the marshes is there, cut and jig-sawed together to a carpet for a deck-chair or a court for thumb-nail tennis. But the life of the suburbs, vast as it is, is still the life of a minority. Out in the provinces, in industrial towns and in the countryside, on the long coasts, in the mountains and islands, and even in the heart of London, are people who still speak with something of the old vitality and splendour. Behind the speech of all country folk lies the imagery of the seasons; behind miners, that of the rock and the depths of the earth; behind sailors, that of the sea. Moreover, there are still millions of people whose lives and language are continually brushed by poetry, little as they may be aware of it; still people who keep hidden beneath the rubbish of commonplace and triviality a small hoard where the imagination can turn over its memories like gold coins.

In my own town, in the drab slate houses, behind the plots of soil where the royal fern grows dusty with the summer, beneath the smoke and the iron, there are men to whom the psalms are banners, and the great myths that trumpeted for Bunyan and Milton are like the sound of a brass band coming faintly, but still distinctly, across distant roofs. The evangelical movement in England was essentially a popular movement. It threw up Watts, Charles Wesley, Cowper and Christopher Smart as the most articulate voices of a choir which was as loud and universal as the sea. Throughout the eighteenth and nineteenth centuries English nonconformity created (or rather *compiled*) for itself an enormous mythological jungle, hot and fertile with emotion, dark with mystery, in which the Rose of Sharon, the lily and the gopher tree grew, and wild, missionary prophets ran by cool Siloam's shady rill. Those of us who were in contact with Methodism in our childhood can remember how this mythology and imagery could descend on a man like Pentecostal fire till he burned with elemental poetry. Indeed, in those parts where tradition stays strongest, in Durham, for instance, and in Wales, there are still people who can remember those to whom the ' gift of tongues ' was given, so that they spoke in a language of their own invention, an evangelical Jabberwocky.

I use the example of Methodism because it made a great impression on my own boyhood. There must, however, be many other ways and modes of life where the speech of the people is enriched with natural rhetoric which draws from the imagery and symbols of a commonly-shared experience. Many poets—Mr. Dylan Thomas, for instance—have drawn on such associations for what one might call a private poetry, but I believe it may also be used as the basis of a verse which shall be close enough to contemporary speech to maintain the illusion of realism, yet can be heightened and re-inforced with the full power and pride of poetry. The Irish have already succeeded in developing from their native speech a diction which may be used with rich embroidery, as in Synge, with plain naturalism, as in Denis Johnstone, or, as in Sean O'Casey, with both at once.

When the poet has evolved his language and found a form in which to speak he must then go out to his audience. That audience, I am sure, is waiting. I cannot speak for London, for I know little of the London theatre, but I have sat with many Northern audiences, and I feel that these people will not be afraid of poetry nor embarrassed by it if the poet will speak in a language which they can understand and which belongs to the life they know.

William Chappell

THE SKULL AND THE IVY LEAVES

A Picture of the Romantic Ballet

THE GHOST of a waltz whispering in the high cornice of a Gothic ballroom. . . .

Ruined archways, through whose crumbling and fretted stonework, the sharp stars of midnight shine. . . .

A delicate hand, idly waving a fan of white peacock feathers that stirs, with a small wind, the damp leaves of ivies trailing in a terraced garden. . . .

A monk's cowl, lifted to reveal in its shadow the equine smile of a skull. . . .

A mask. . . .

A heart, breaking for love. . . .

These, the trappings of dreams, the pictures that might take shape behind the eyes of one who leans from a high window and stares out across a darkening landscape, are the pattern of the fabric of the Romantic Ballet.

Though many years lie between ' Giselle ', and the ' Lilac Gardens ', the ' Apparitions ', of our contemporary ballet, they are all informed with a similar feeling, spring from one source, and seem, one might say, to be heavy with the perfume of moon-drenched flowers. Nearly all of them are pre-occupied with betrayal, frustration, or death, which accords ill with the accepted idea of the spirit of English art; and yet this pre-occupation, which produced such beautiful poetry in the generation which followed Keats is still indisputably present in one of its aspects today, the ballet.

This motif of romantic feeling, so frequently recurring in present day choreographic trends, is there not only because the choreographers have instinctively discovered an urge for it themselves; the ballet public has also shown a hunger for, and a response to, romanticism, that can only be explained by the existence of some emotional need.

During a great part of the twentieth century, the world has been more than usually aware of death in the many violent and horrifying forms it takes in great wars and revolutions. The fact that the great majority of human beings, even the poorest and unhappiest, dread death, makes it perhaps, consoling to see it tricked out like a dream; and in the ballet, as in all manifestations of the Romantic movement in art, the vision of death is disguised in a way that gives it a bitter sweet magical beauty. The maggots are half concealed by full-blown roses; the bony hand lies within a jewelled glove; the skeleton's hollow ribs are veiled with gauze, and the skull is hidden behind a mask and a fan. Death, perhaps, could be like that? So, something within us is satisfied when we see ' Giselle ' and ' Apparitions '.

We know that poverty is sad, cruel, and ugly. Therefore it is pleasant to be persuaded that it can be decorative and moving, delicately coloured and subtly shaped, as in ' Les Forains ', a ballet in the modern romantic idiom, that has grown directly from the renaissance of romanticism which came about in the nineteen thirties. The dinginess of present day existence creates, in each of us, a need to clothe misery in a pictorial imagery that may help to make it appear more palatable. This need can be satisfied by the visions of the romantic movement in the ballet, giving us those pictures that are lit by unreal lingering sunsets, by the blue jewelled moon of the limelights; those enchanted figures that die so gently, with such grace, whose hearts break to music, whose melancholy and madness are always visually beautiful.

The growth of the Romantic Ballet has been consecutive and logical, and though there may appear to be no connection in feeling between the Gothic dream world of ' Giselle ' or ' La Sylphide ', and the pure abstractions of ' Symphonic Variations ', they are, nevertheless, links at the beginning and the end of the same chain. Ashton's ballet has shown a contemporary romanticism, based only on movement, and the juxtaposition of bodies that remain sexless and serene, afloat in a spatial geometry, bound by the curved lines of Sophie Fedorovitch's exquisitely apt décor.

If I should be taken sharply to task for setting ' Symphonic Variations ' in the sequences of the Romantic Ballet, I can only, in self-defence, say that the appeal of works such as ' Giselle ', ' La Sylphide ', ' Symphonie Fantasque ', and ' Apparitions ', is at bottom, for me the same emotional appeal as that of ' Symphonic Variations ', which expresses, in some inexplicable abstract way, as much, or even more, of the human heart, as any ballet with a definite plot or obvious theme.

Between this work, and the rich crowded pictures created by the mid-nineteenth-century ballets, it is fairly simple to trace how we arrived at a point where the angle of a dancer's head can induce tears in the onlooker, and the cool beauty of six figures, like human planets revolving on some preordained plan in inter-stellar space, can stir our emotions so deeply.

The death wish, the morbid melancholy fascination of gravestones, coffins, wicked monks, and ivy-clad ruins, repeats itself, either in actuality, or atmosphere, over and over again from the early days, to appear as lately as in the Howard–Stevenson ' Mardi-Gras ' and in Petit's ' La Fiancée du Diable '—the Gothic to end all Gothick. Among the contemporary ballets of the last twenty years, we can follow a new line, when the old symbols are gradually discarded, and fresh ones appear, leading us from Nijinska's ' La Bien-Aimée ' via Balanchine's ' Cotillons ', to Ashton's ' The Wanderer ', where we have left the earth we know and crept inside the brain of the poet from ' Apparitions ' to find ourselves in a new landscape, a bleak, withered lunar region. Yet the figures that people this desolate country have their counterparts in other romantic ballets. It is on the tip of our tongues to say: ' I don't remember the name—but the face is familiar '. Without doubt, it is familiar; the femme du monde, the young lovers, the hero, who is poet, visionary, musician, or benighted traveller; and the chorus, who have been monks, devils, witches or carnival grotesques, and are now menacing disembodied darknesses; every character in ' The Wanderer ' is a contemporary expression of an eternal romantic type.

Ashton's ' Nocturne ', with its impersonal onlooker and its 'nineties beauties, brilliant as a bouquet of anemones, was a half-way house between ' Apparitions ' and ' The Wanderer '. Its characters derive their being from the romantic period; the innocent beautiful flower girl, the dashing hero-villain (Albrecht and Hilarion in one) and the glittering woman and her cavaliers, but the ballet has shed the Gothic atmosphere, and while the symbols used are more delicate—a posy of violets, the long white gloves of some Edwardian gala at the opera— the story is true to type, with its innocent love, betrayal, and despair.

The next step had to be an expression of frustration and tragedy no longer individual, formed instead to embrace all humanity. To convey this, Ashton produced ' Dante Sonata '. Once more the death wish, and at the same time the old romanticism, the powers of evil, the lovers torn asunder, the crucifixion symbols, the corpse; only, unlike the original romantic works where love must triumph, even if it has to be after death, in ' Dante Sonata ' pity is equally distributed on good and evil. Both suffer. Both are frustrated. Both are crucified.

From this ballet, in which the bodies of the dancers form the symbols of despair, of love and death, it is easy to follow the evolution of a modern romanticism revealed in the serene purity of ' Symphonic Variations ' where male and female have become almost as impersonal as electrons; yet, as they revolve round one another, forming a continual harmonious design, they seem to express the secret of all existence.

To take only Ashton's ballets as an example of progression in the Romantic School, would be to show merely one side of the choreographic picture. It is simple to trace the movement we are studying, in his choreography, his line and his approach being so essentially romantic and his development so clear from one work to another.

But there is a clarity of progression in the work of other living dance designers, and Antony Tudor has shown in his ' Pillar of Fire ', a remarkable example of a contemporary approach to the old themes of romanticism. Anyone who has followed this choreographer's work from his days with Marie Rambert, will understand how ' Pillar of Fire ' grew quite naturally from qualities present in two of his earlier ballets, the straightforward emotions of ' Lilac Garden ' and the abstract emotions of ' Dark Elegies '. These two conceptions fuse easily and beautifully in the later ballet.

Frustration is its principal theme, as it is in greater or lesser degree the theme of almost every romantic ballet, and it is true to tradition that frustration and heart-break should be vanquished in the final picture, as the lovers, eternally united, move away from us through green transparent woods, behind the floating unattached figures of the corps de ballet, who are so typical of this choreographer's style.

To some, ' Pillar of Fire ' may appear to be as out of place in the Romantic repertoire as ' Symphonic Variations '. Actually, I believe it to belong there with even clearer right, not simply because it is fundamentally true to type, with good and evil characters strongly contrasted, and unrequited love as a mainspring for its action, but, above all, because it has a sustained emotional strength and a physical intensity overlaid by poetry, giving it the quality that sets a Romantic ballet truly in its own genre.

This poetical, moving appeal, this intensity is found in each one of the ballets I have mentioned, giving them a kinship, whether they be truly Gothic, rich with symbols, or scorn any symbolic decoration other than that conceived by the choreographer in terms of his dancers' limbs and bodies.

Andrée Howard is another English choreographer who delights in the sentiments and trappings of the Romantic period; and yet, though she is highly gifted, and possesses taste and sensitivity, she somehow fails to belong as completely as one might expect to this particular group. In approach, she would appear to be one of the most obvious candidates for membership of the Romantic school. The subjects and settings of her ballets are heavily endowed with signs and portents that we recognise. Masks, gloves, fans and plumes. . . . Coffins, corpses, moonlight, candlelight and shadows. . . . Muses. . . . Young girls and men who move, quietly as a sigh, in a tranced world. . . .

But her choreographic movement is so tenuous and hesitant that, finally, her ballets lack strength in emotion, a full blooded romantic feeling, and as a result their content rarely seems to justify their length.

' Fête Etrange ' is in some ways, quite exquisite, and the impact of its first few minutes on the senses, is genuinely haunting, but how much is due to the choreographer and how much to its designer it is not easy to say. Its mysterious twilight lit by the spectre of a crystal chandelier, that, afloat in the dusk of a winter's evening, drops a faint tinkling music on to the snow-covered terraces of the gardens where the action takes place. The delicately luminous figures who move so sweetly and silently, no word, no laughter, only a half smile, as they meet and part, revolving round the bewildered dreaming boy-child who has strayed amongst them. The unknown beauty, and the sombre handsome man who watches her from the icy terrace. These are, or should be, the very breath of romanticism. But the movement and the conception are so frail, so understated, they fail to hold the attention, and catch neither the heart nor the eye, though decoratively this work is another triumph for Sophie Fedorovitch. As choreography it is as though one had dreamed it, and waking, one could hardly remember anything about it. It is the ghost of a Romantic ballet.

Andrée Howard is on firmer ground with ' Mardi-Gras ', even if we are back with ' Apparitions ' and ' Symphonie Fantasque '. It is a re-statement, not a new vision, and for those who love the Romantic period it has the expected pleasures. The atmosphere of death. The phosphorescence of decay. The familiar macabre thrill of the open coffin in which the trembling heroine knows she will see her own self lying, pallid with heavy-lidded eyes.

Corpse must join hand with ivy-wreathed spirit; masked woman in ball gown of gauze must link fingers with the evil Queen of the Wilis. Poets, wild with melancholy, embrace skeletons, pressing fevered kisses on hands that are only bone, while about them and about, a whirling silent multitude of figures, monks in purple and scarlet habits, sinister revellers garbed in grey, white and silver, black witches, mocking Pun-chinellos, move wildly from steely moonlight to the indigo shadows of tombs and ruins.

Like planets with attendant constellations, certain radiant shapes revolve serenely across and through the writhing tortured crowds. It is the Romantic ballet.

5

Raymond Queneau

THE PRINCE FROM POLDAVIA

Translated from the French by J. Maclaren Ross

FOR THE past two years Pierrot had lived in the same hotel. It'd become a habit. Hotel de l'Aveyron, a lightly built structure with only one floor, and a balcony on the outside which formed a means of communication between the various rooms. The courtyard had once been a farmyard, the attic-window looked out onto the garden of a convent. Pierrot's neighbour was an old workman, very quiet, never spoke. Further away there were some couples, who looked after themselves. The proprietor didn't care about anything much. The slatternly servant had never tried to seduce Pierrot. She wasn't too bad-looking, for that matter. Pierrot liked his digs fine.

The day after his second expulsion from the Amusement Park he got up quite late for him, about seven, having lain awake in bed. He carefully washed any part of himself that might have smelt unwholesome, wet his hair, brushed it down with his hands, wiped his shoes on the turn-ups of his trousers; now he's ready, now he's standing before a steaming cup on a counter, he reads a racing paper to pick out the little gee-gee on which he'll later risk a couple of coins, he'll think about that all morning, it's only eight so far.

He went up into his room again. The floor had been swept and the bed made. Pierrot spread out the racing paper so's not to dirty the eiderdown and then lay down. He smoked. He waited for the time to pass. All the men had gone to work. The housewives chattered among themselves. Cars purred up the street, little girls were playing in the convent garden. Everything very peaceful.

From time to time Pierrot shut his eyes. Ten minutes, a quarter of an hour leapt by like that. When he opened his eyes nothing had changed. Then he took up another cigarette and puffed the smoke slowly towards the ceiling. A large sunbeam lay in front of the window, which was open on the balcony. Big bluebottles buzzed in, then buzzed out again angrily. Little flies were strolling about everywhere. The housewives had gone to the market, the playground of the convent was empty, traffic rumbled some way off. Everything changed bit by bit with the passage of time.

At half nine Pierrot got up, folded his racing paper, and got going. It was quite a way from his hotel to the Amusement Park: he went on foot. He walked slowly, hardly lifting the soles of his shoes from the asphalt. He stopped to look in shops, furniture shops whose owners had country-houses, shops that sold stamps, shops that sold bicycles, shops that sold papers, garages. He took care not to miss the man who made ball-bearings, who showed in his window little steel spheres bouncing mathematically on tambourines of the same metal. Then he went up the Avenue de Chaillot, and there in front of him was the Amusement Park: its monumental gateway supported by naked women in pink stucco, with fuzzy hair, huge breasts and wide hips; the scaffolding of the Scenic Railway; the Pisa-like tower of the Chair-o'-Planes. Without hurrying he passed by the closed gate, by the wall of the Dance Pavilion, then turned right into the Rue des Larmes, by the side-gate, also closed.

He'd never been in this street before. Some garages and cafés occupied its left side, also a villa that must have dated from the days of Louis Philippe. On the other side the wall of the Amusement Park stopped twenty yards from the Avenue de Chaillot. Farther along, separated from the street by a grille, there was a sort of chapel, in a kind of square. Pierrot took no interest in this at first. He did sentry-go, eagerly watching the end of the street, where Yvonne might appear. But Yvonne didn't show up. When noon struck it began to look as if she wasn't coming that day.

Pierrot then noticed a man coming out of the Louis Philippe-looking villa; who locked the door behind him; who crossed the road; and, with a second key, unlocked the grille; walked across the square; then with a third key opened the door of the chapel, it certainly seemed to be a chapel, but of a kind unknown to Pierrot, who was in any case no church-crawler. The man went into the chapel. The door shut behind him. Pierrot was interested. He thought he might have a look. Finally he went across, but the man was coming out at that moment. So Pierrot said:

'Excuse me, sir, could you tell me——'

But the other interrupted:

'Are you a Poldavian, young man?'

'Me? No. In fact, I don't know what a——'

'Just a busybody, then?'

'Well, I was just passing, sir, and——'

'Now, now, young man, d'you mean to say you don't know what this chapel is?'

'I'm afraid I don't, sir.'

'Well, of course it's not very well known. There are books that would tell you all about it, but they're very learned and only to be found in museums.'

'I don't get much time for reading.'

'I am not reproaching you with that fact, young man. So you just asked yourself what this chapel could be, eh?'

'Yes, sir. I'm sorry if——'

'Not at all, but——'

He took a gold hunter from his pocket and looked at the time.

'—it's time for my lunch. Another time. Au revoir, young man.'

And he crossed the road. Opening with his first key the door of his house, he went in.

In front of a garage, some workmen were arguing the toss. Pierrot approached the group and inquired politely of the origins and nature of that little monument over there, in the square.

'Search me, mate,' said one.

'What's it got to do with you, anyway?' asked another.

'It's a chapel,' answered a third. 'To get in, you got to ask the bloke that lives opposite.'

'Go on?' said the other two admiringly, astounded by the extent of his knowledge.

They started all at once to take notice of this thingummy they'd never noticed until now.

Pierrot thanked them for the information. Then he went towards the Universal Bar, a café well known in the neighbourhood, on the corner facing Pradonet's house. The gaffers from the Amusement Park used it; a cigarette counter and a totalisator attracted a good clientele; female camp-followers used it as a post of observation and information; the sandwiches were good. Pierrot ordered one, that had ham in it, with lots of butter and mustard, and, as was the custom, poured white wine over it. He hoped to see Paradis, who wasn't there. Then, biting into his lunch, he went across to the tote. Too late, he might've known. On the programme he looked for his horse and wasn't sorry he'd failed to back it. He turned towards a pin-table and put a coin in the slot. Soon there was an admiring circle round him. It was marvellous to see the steel balls following their appointed course, rolling down paths obstructed by the most cunning devices, falling into place, ringing bells, lighting the machine up like a Christmas tree. Pierrot made 22,000 on his first game, 7,000 more than he needed to have a buckshee go. On the second he reached 30,000; on the third he went back to 16,000; on the fourth he climbed again to 31,000. All this for a franc. He'd finished his sandwich and left the game to anybody else who wasn't afraid to look silly playing after him.

'Well, well, my boy, you seem to be in form.'

Pierrot thought he recognised that voice, but he wasn't sure. He drank his white wine unhurriedly, then:

'I do my best,' he said modestly.

'What's your worst—sending your boss flying arse over tip?' replied Pradonet.

'How much do I owe you?' Pierrot asked the waiter.

'Don't run away, I won't hurt you. Ha! ha! ha! That was a hell of a joke to play on me, that was. Ha! ha!'

Pierrot pocketed his change, wondering how he could escape.

'I recognised you,' Pradonet insisted. 'I've a memory for faces. And what're you doing now?'

'I'm down the pan,' Pierrot told him resolutely.

Pradonet examined him for several seconds in silence, then:

'I feel bad about you, you know.'

He turned towards an individual with an air as distinguished as his beard, who stood behind him:

'Here's a boy who'd suit you,' he said.

'All right,' said Crouia Bey, 'but he'll have to take his glasses off.'

'What's the job?' asked Pierrot.

'You'll be dressed up as a hindu,' said the fakir. 'I've got the costume, and you'll hand me what I need with respectful gestures. I'll show you how to do it. I'll make you up, too.'

'How's that suit you?' asked Pradonet. 'You'll be in the first gaff on the right, beyond the pay-box.'

'Be there tonight at eight,' added Crouia Bey.

'But they'll never let me in,' said Pierrot.

'I'll give 'em orders to,' said Pradonet, 'but no more passes at my daughter, mind, or else. What you do outside's your own business. I don't give a sod. But not in working hours, understand?'

'Thank you, sir,' said Pierrot.

'See you this evening,' said Crouia Bey.

'How much do I get?' asked Pierrot.

'Ten francs a night,' said Crouia Bey.

'What, all night?' asked Pierrot.

'Yes,' said Crouia Bey.

'Twenty francs then,' said Pierrot.

Pradonet began to laugh.

'The boy's got guts.'

And to the fakir:

'Go on, give him fifteen.'

'I won't argue,' said Crouia Bey, 'but it comes out of my salary. However, since you say so——'

To Pierrot:

'All right, fifteen. Tonight at eight.'

The two men went off, Pradonet pleased as punch, the fakir plainly peeved. Pierrot went out after them, keeping his distance. Coming back up the Rue des Larmes he looked at the house and the chapel, but didn't dare go near them. Then he thought he'd look at the Seine, and turned in that direction. He walked nonchalantly, as was his habit, thinking less about his new job than about the significance of that small monument.

A few yards away from the customs-house he passed by an old café; a game of billiards was dragging to a close inside; on the terrace, consisting of two or three iron tables and chairs, he saw that man again, drinking a beer. He went across.

'Well, well,' said the guardian of the chapel, 'looking for me, young man?'

'Not at all,' Pierrot told him, 'it's only by chance that I——'

'But you look very pleased to see me again, all the same.'

'It'd be difficult for me to contradict you, sir, but——'

'Why don't you sit down, young man?'

Pierrot sat down. A waitress came and asked him what he'd have; the old boy finished his beer rapidly and ordered two more:

'Curiosity must have sharpened your wits,' he said. 'You ran me to earth straight away.'

'But I assure you that I wasn't——'

'Don't attempt to deny it, now. In any case what does it matter? Although curiosity certainly killed the cat——'

Pierrot got up:

'I wouldn't like you to think——'

'Sit down.'

Pierrot sat down.

'I'm going to tell you the story of my life,' the old man said.

'What about the chapel?' asked Pierrot.

'Listen and don't interrupt.'

He coughed three times and then told the following story:

'I was born in that house which you saw in the Rue des Larmes, where I have always lived. In those days long, long ago, the Rue des Larmes was only a cart-track, barely negotiable in winter, and the Amusement Park didn't exist. There was nothing in the neighbourhood but waste land, small workshops, stables, workmen's huts, unsalubrious enterprises, horse-dealers, farms and the like. It was an evil neighbourhood: one was always coming across women cut to bits or informers with their throats slit. We used to bolt ourselves in at night; my father had a shot-gun. Sometimes I'd hear screams in the night, enough to make you shiver. I couldn't sleep a wink.

' My father was a great big hulking man about six feet tall, and the last member of an old family from Argenteuil, who at one time owned most of the land between the fortifications and the Seine, in this part of Paris. And the ground on which the Amusement Park now stands belonged to him too. Well, nowadays I suppose you would look on him as a failure, but that did not seem to stop him from being happy, despite, of course, a few regrets. He had imagined himself to be an artist; he wanted to become a painter, but he only succeeded in getting a model with child, my mother, who afterwards became an excellent woman of the utmost modesty. It was thus that I knew her, thus that I saw her die.

' Having knocked about doing nothing for some time, my father eventually found his real métier: modelling in wax. The busts modelled by him were exhibited both in fairgrounds and in anatomical museums. He was the best known maker of waxworks in Paris: he could do a wonderful likeness and no one knew better how to reproduce, from the material at his disposal, the peculiar abnormalities of the human body or the corruption that flesh is heir to. I have already told you that the neighbourhood we lived in was hardly reassuring: the house itself now became even worse. Although I was never allowed in my father's studio, I would stumble from time to time, when I was least expecting them, upon decapitated heads that turned my stomach upside down. And when, in bed at night, I heard a noise or a strangled scream for help, I would imagine that a dead man, still warm and stained with his own blood, had crept into the house to lead the infernal choir of waxwork figures. Lying there, I used to sweat with fear.

' So, from the age of thirteen onward, I did all I could to persuade my parents to apprentice me to a trade. I gladly left that house of terror, but what I went to was in a way more terrible. You can have no idea what it was like to be an apprentice half a century ago, and since life was hard enough for grown working-men, it was sheer misery for a lad of fifteen. How I began to regret the life I had left behind me, but it was far too late for recrimination; I had to undergo these hardships, working without pause for breath, starving for lack of food. And my military service, when I was called up, seemed, by comparison, a wonderful holiday. Ah, what memories! To have friends and comrades, to travel in foreign lands. . . . I did my time in North Africa, young man, and in the Hussars to boot—a fine regiment. I very nearly signed on for good. But at the last moment I became ill of a tropical fever and was sent home.

' Hardly anything had changed during my absence. There were more workmen's shelters, more allotments, and in the waste lands young hooligans were playing games. At the corner of the Avenue Chaillot, a greyhound track had grown up, and attracted a mixed clientele of ragamuffins, dog-fanciers and rich sportsmen. But at night all this reverted to a mournful silence, and only the cries of people being set upon and murdered detracted from the utter stillness pervading the spot. Our old house was still standing: I was never to leave it again. I learned to model from my father: I was a man now and had seen worse things than wax-work figures: in any case my father had given up the manufacture of anatomical pieces in favour of portraiture, and busts of great men. It was in this branch of the art that I was to carry on my father's tradition, which I never let down.

'My father, I need not tell you, was of a saturnine and gloomy temperament, which I have in part inherited. Perhaps solar or mercurial influences prevented me as a child from taking pleasure in the sight of purulent chancres or children born with calves' heads. But it was not long before I began to like solitude, the life of a recluse, my pipe, and to frequent the society of women from houses of ill-fame, when the need took me. In fact I adopted the habits of a confirmed bachelor. I never married, although I loved several women madly: an Arab dancing girl, for whose sake I almost became a Muslim; later, a female butcher in the Avenue Chaillot. You know that people following that trade have a peculiar rich texture of skin all their own. Anyhow, neither one nor the other made me long to pass all my days on this earth in their company.

'My father died a few months after the death of my mother. It was afterwards that I learned to appreciate and to savour the bittersweetness of a solitary life. As I've already said, I never got married. I told you also that my family owned all this part of the city right up to the Seine. But when my father was the only member left alive, all that remained to him was our house on one side of the road and on the other the piece of ground occupied at present by the Amusement Park—and by the chapel. You may have noticed that the ground adjoining this takes the form of a rectangle. It is the site of a vegetable garden that my father had planted there. Shortly after his death a man came and suggested that I should sell him the property I'd inherited. I hesitated. He offered me what was a large sum of money for those days. I gave way, but I kept for my own use the vegetable garden, promising to let him have the first offer if I ever decided to sell. Life went on as before, except that I now had a little money, and did not have to worry about my old age, for I had invested the money in gilt-edged securities, both here and abroad. As for the garden, I went on cultivating it assiduously.

'Well, one morning as I was tending my lettuces (I had a lovely crop that summer, twenty years ago—I was just entering into my fiftieth year); it was in June, a crude fierce sun had just risen over the roofs of Paris, a heat haze shimmered over the Bois de Boulogne—suddenly I heard a horse galloping, then a cry. My garden was enclosed by a little wooden fence, through which the horse had crashed, and its rider was flung from the saddle, falling like a thunderbolt into the middle of my vegetable garden.

'He lay still.

'I rushed forward. He had fainted. He seemed to be half-dead. I called for help. Neighbours ran up. They went to fetch a doctor, the police, and an ambulance. The injured man was carried away. In the meantime he had recovered consciousness and expressed the wish to go home. Next day I learned from the papers that he had died soon afterwards. I learned from them also that he was none other than Prince Luigi Voudzoi, a Poldavian prince, finishing his studies in France, though the rumour had it that these studies consisted principally of drinking and gaming.

'The funeral took place some days later. I went to it. It was a wonderful funeral, very picturesque and moving. They buried the Prince in Père Lachaise, and after the ceremony I stayed there until the evening, dreaming from those heights that look down upon our capital. I continued to tend my lettuces, but while cultivating my garden I couldn't help thinking about that accident: the most important event in my life, apart from my service in North Africa. It had made me famous in the neighbourhood, and I found myself obliged to recount the story several times every day. Soon I was seized with a desire to know more about Poldavian history; this people, according to the papers, lived in a far-away mountain region. I borrowed books from the public library, and then I discovered that I couldn't understand history without a knowledge of chronology and geography, which did not seem to me comprehensible without astronomy and cosmography, and astronomy and cosmography I could not fully appreciate without a knowledge of arithmetic and geometry. I therefore started my education *ab ovo*, which means right from the beginning, in Latin (how much more economical and expressive—you see, young man, the advantages of a classical education). At the end of several months I had learned once again the rules of grammar, the formulæ of compound interest, crucial dates in French history, the location of the Great Bear, and many passages from the classics.

'So the summer and the autumn passed. Then one day as I was sitting outside my door to profit by the declining sun, I noticed a very well-dressed young gentleman who seemed to be looking for something. He approached and asked very courteously if I could not show him the exact spot where a noble foreigner had met a violent death some months previously. "Nothing is easier," said I, "for I was the only witness of the unfortunate accident. It took place facing you," I added, "in that little vegetable garden opposite, which belongs to me." "Would it not be possible for you to show me the spot itself? " he asked me. He quickly added that, if this were not convenient, he would come back another time; and he asked me to believe that it was not out of vulgar curiosity that he was putting me to this small trouble. He had a very good reason, and to convince me of his *bona fides* he gave me his name and title, which he thought would be sufficient, and in this supposition he was correct. There stood before me a Poldavian prince. " Prince," said I, " I will not hesitate to perform this sacred duty," and I escorted him to the bed of lettuces into which the other had been thrown to his death. Two simple wooden crosses, one for his head, the other for his feet, marked the spot. This was the method I had chosen of commemorating this remarkable event. The Prince was touched by this little attention, and a tear coursed down his cheek. Then he knelt down in prayer, and stayed for some minutes in meditation beside the spot. I respected his silence and stood to a sort of moral attention, waiting for him to address me again. Which he did, in these words:

' " Did I understand you to tell me," said he, " that this garden belongs to you? " " Yes, Prince," I answered. " You also own the ground around it? " " Yes, Prince," I answered. " Would you be good enough to tell me your name? " " Arteme Mounnezergues," I answered. " And you live——? " " In that house opposite, Prince," I answered. " And you were present at Prince Luigi's accident? " " Yes, Prince," I answered, " I was the only witness." Then he asked me to tell him exactly what I had observed on the morning of the tragedy. I obeyed at once, with pleasure. The Prince listened with the gravest attention, and when I had concluded my story he assured me that the Poldavian princes would never forget the delicacy of sentiment expressed by the two crosses which I had planted in the garden. He added two words only: " Thank you," and climbed into a carriage which, no doubt, had brought him there but which I had not noticed. The carriage drove away.

' After this visit I was all the more anxious to make a closer acquaintance with the Poldavian people and their princes. I could now see quite clearly that the spot marked out by me was evidently a fateful one. The plants withered in its neighbourhood, the grubs which crawled over them died suddenly, and I found the remains of charred caterpillars on the leaves. And I realised then that this spot was set apart from all others, over-shadowed as it was by the disembodied spirit of what had happened. The window of my room overlooked the garden and although at night I could see no ghost floating there, silvered by the moonbeams, I told myself, nevertheless, that never again could carrots, turnips, lettuces or cucumbers be grown upon this tragic site. And I stood rapt.

'Years passed, and long after the visit of which I have just spoken, I was honoured by the receipt of a singular missive. I was not a little surprised that morning to see the postman entering my gate. No one ever wrote to me. The envelope was large, the notepaper inside of the thickest, and crested, moreover, with the arms of Poldavia, " de sable a l'orle de huit larmes d'argent." I was invited to come to a certain hotel in the Latin quarter next day at five p.m. I went. After having submitted to a most searching examination from the caretaker, I was shown up to the room. It was very small and dark. The Prince was lying on his bed smoking. Near him stood a bottle and two glasses. He signed to me to sit in the chair opposite him and poured out with his own hand a large measure of the raki which he himself was drinking. This reminded me of North Africa, but I dared not ask if he were acquainted with that country. To have done so would have been disrespectful. I attended carefully to my host. This was the gist of his speech. " Sir," said he, " the princes of Poldavia have decided to erect a monument on the very spot where Luigi fell to his death. We wish to establish a lasting memorial to this sad event, and in order to do so, as you will understand, it is necessary for that piece of ground which is yours to become our property. I am therefore authorised to ask you at what price you would consent to sell your vegetable garden." After all the thought I had given to the subject of fateful spots, of which I have already spoken, it will not astonish you to learn that I was partly prepared for this proposition. I might even add that I felt at once a sort of relief, but I had to think of my previous commitments. I attempted to explain to my host that I had already promised the sale of this ground, eventually, to the gentleman who had bought my other property. The Prince hastened to dispel my scruples. Was it not a case of *force majeure*? How could one compare this natural wish on the part of the Poldavian princes with the mechanical fulfilment of a contract which was not even a contract, since it was little more than a promise, or not even a promise, but a conditional agreement? Was I going to put difficulties in the way of an act of piety on the pretext of satisfying the rapacity of a buyer wishing to own all the property within his reach? No, of course not.

'I consented then to sell the ground, but I soon realised that my host was unable to pay cash. He proposed a system of payments on the instalment plan, which would cover a number of years, and which would also reimburse me for the time and trouble which would be my lot as guardian of the monument that they wished to erect. Finally we came to terms.

'The building was embarked upon immediately and, in less than six months, a chapel erected on the spot. Then Prince Luigi's remains were exhumed from Père Lachaise and laid in the tomb.

'Thanks to the sale of the ground which I had inherited and to the instalments paid to me by the Poldavian princes I was enabled to continue my studies, which I directed principally towards history, ancient and modern, physical and political geography, pure and applied mathematics, the main languages, both dead and alive, physical and natural science, rhetoric and theology. I had two or three years of peace. Then all of a sudden the Amusement Park came into being, insolently clamouring for attention. It was sacrilegious, I told myself, to install a pleasure-ground so close to a tomb. I made representations to the owner, one Pradonet, but he for his part found the proximity of this circumscribed cemetery lugubrious and ill-omened. He proposed to buy back the garden and return Prince Luigi to Père Lachaise. I refused. He became angry. There the matter rested. Since then he has several times made the same proposition to me. I have always rejected it, although in the meantime the situation has somewhat changed. In fact, two or three years after the building of the chapel, the instalments from Poldavia ceased abruptly. Nobody knew where the princes were, or who they were. Thus it is that I became once again the owner of the garden, remaining, however, the guardian of the tomb.

'That is my story and that of the chapel. What is the chapel? The mausoleum of a Poldavian prince, without heirs or vassals. What am I? A self-appointed and faithful custodian. One final point: the reason why the street in which I live is called the Rue des Larmes is because the municipal authorities so named it in honour of the Poldavian princes, in whose crest tears figure so largely.'

Mounnezergues emptied his half-pint.

'Thank you, sir,' said Pierrot, 'for giving me this information, but really it was not idle curiosity which——'

'I quite understand. No one knows more about the hazards of life than I. Twenty years ago there was no indication that, on the waste land overlooked by my windows, would one day rise the bizarre and garish buildings which make up the Amusement Park, and that I would save from their encroaching cancer a plot of earth where, in a precarious peace, lies the young and noble victim of a tragic accident. Even less would I have foreseen my fate when, in the uniform of the 3rd Hussars, I counted the stars in the African sky; and before that, when I was a child terrorised by waxwork figures and the cries of lost souls, no oracle could have foretold that I would pass my old age watching over the sepulchre of a Poldavian prince.'

Pierrot nodded pensively. His glass was empty.

'Another?' suggested Mounnezergues.

'No, thank you, sir. I have to go. I've got to buy something.'

Mounnezergues was indulgent towards white lies. He paid for the drinks after several tentative attempts on the part of Pierrot, and let him go where he pleased. Pierrot thanked the old man once again, and they separated, the one returning to his house, the other walking down towards the river.

The river was not more than ten minutes away from the fortifications, from which it was separated by a region given up to manufacturers of coffee-mills, aeroplane factories and garages for the repair of various types of vehicle. The straight broad road was only paved in places, grass grew between the stones while the machines hummed. The Avenue Chaillot ran parallel, a peaceful thoroughfare. At the end of it was the Seine, with its fishing-boats and fishermen.

Pierrot's mind was a blank as he walked along; it needed no especial effort on his part to bring about this state of affairs: it was habitual to him. Thus he arrived on the quay. Traffic noises could be heard from the Route Nationale. The river bank was overgrown with dusty but thriving plants. The fish were biting. Pierrot sat down and lit a cigarette. He watched the static straw hats of the anglers and the fishing lines which drifted with the current, or were sometimes jerked brusquely into the air. A sewer emptied itself, tainting the deep fresh water. In green painted boats, fanatical figures crouched over their rods as though turned to stone.

Pierrot was not especially interested in the scene before him. He was indifferent to it. He had come there, not for distraction, but to conjure up the image of Yvonne.

Since the age of twelve Pierrot had been in love hundreds of times; sometimes he'd even met with success, but this was something quite different: a new country of love to be explored, with limitless frontiers and boundless possibilities. Although he'd had a wide enough experience of women, without, however, straying very far from the street corner, he'd never come across anyone in the least like Yvonne, except, perhaps, women he'd seen on the screen. She was rather like them, come to think of it, with her blonde hair, her hollow cheeks, the way she swayed her hips. He'd tell her that, she might be pleased. Pierrot shut his eyes, remembering the chatter of the Dodgems track, the dynamic speed of the little vehicle in which she'd pressed against him; the scent which surrounded her seemed once more to tickle his nostrils, his heart turned over and he almost swooned at the memory of the luscious perfume which lent sex appeal to her woman's sweat.

He reopened his eyes. The Seine flowed by, calm and grey. The static straw hats were bowed over their sterile rods. A mongrel dog rolled happily in a pile of dung. Over on the Route Nationale motor-cars and lorries were passing.

Pierrot inhaled a lungful of air. He was still knocked all of a heap. Decidedly this was a grand passion, the real thing, true love. He lit a fresh cigarette from the butt of the previous one, which he had put down near him, and thought things over seriously. He was hooked all right, no doubt about that. But the first thing to do was to meet her again. He chewed this thought over like tender grass, without, however, formulating any definite and practical plan of campaign. Towards the end of the afternoon he got up, stretched and yawned. He was not, however, any further advanced, except that he meant to go back to the Rue des Larmes next morning, in the hope of seeing her again. For the moment to be in love was enough. He retraced his steps vaguely whistling a tune he couldn't remember the name of, but which, had he been more musical, he might have recognised as the song diffused by the amplifier on the Dodgems track while he was circling round and round with the smashing piece he'd just picked up and with whom he was now so taken.

He arrived at the Universal Café with time to spare before reporting to Crouia Bey. Entering, he found Petit Pouce and Paradis sitting there, each with a plate of pickled onions and a big pint of Light in front of him. They'd won on the tote.

'Well, me old cocker,' said Paradis. 'Going to join us?'

'Thanks,' said Pierrot.

'What'll it be?' asked the waitress, funny-looking girl she was.

'A half and a ham sandwich with mustard in,' said Pierrot.

'Bring him pickled onions and a pint,' said Paradis to Fifine, the funny-looking waitress. 'It's on me.'

'You got slung out again last night, so I hear?' said Petit Pouce, intent on consuming, meanwhile, one of the largest onions.

'That's right,' answered Pierrot, laughing, 'but that won't stop me going back again today.'

'What!' exclaimed Petit Pouce.

'How'll you manage that then?' asked Paradis.

Pierrot told them about his new job.

'No, by Christ,' choked Paradis, 'you can't expect us to swallow that.'

Fifine brought more pickled onions and while Pierrot put them away eagerly the others resumed a scientific argument, based on much study of form, about the merits of various gees bound to romp in first and others that might be backed for a place.

Pierrot caught them up on the afters, and Paradis ordered coffee and brandy. Petit Pouce said to Pierrot:

'I hear you been chatting the big boss's daughter?'

'I've only spoken to her twice,' said Pierrot.

'Well, you'd be a b.f. not to make a pass,' said Petit Pouce, 'there've been others before you.'

'You're not one of 'em,' Paradis told him.

'I don't care either way,' said Pierrot, wiping his glasses on a paper napkin.

He grinned stupidly.

Petit Pouce thought he looked like something the cat'd brought in.

'How about a game?' he jerked his thumb towards the pin-table.

'Not tonight,' said Paradis. 'We've no time.'

'I'll come with you,' said Pierrot, putting on his glasses, 'I got to be there at eight.'

Nobody seemed to mind his entering the Amusement Park. One of the bouncers, leaning against the gate, pretended not to see him. Petit Pouce and Paradis left Pierrot, who made for the first gaff on the right, where large posters announced the exploits of Crouia Bey, and described them with the usual superlatives. The posters showed the protagonist with hooks inserted under his shoulder-blades, pulling along a Rolls Royce, or else eating broken bottles and iron bars hot from the fire. Pierrot made a face; this sort of thing revolted him.

He went in the back door. Crouia Bey was there all dressed up, preparing for the performance.

'About time,' he said. 'Put this costume on, here, yes, that's it. Well, go on, shake it up, at the double, what a time to take. Ah, good, at last! Come here so I can black your face. Take off your glasses, then, you b.f. Hold still while I get the paint on, right, that's got it. Quick now, this turban. H'm, well, I suppose that'll have to do; you don't look too bad.'

Then he explained Pierrot's duties in detail. The barker came in to see if they were ready. They were. The barker then switched on the loudspeaker, which blared out Ravel's 'Bolero' at full blast, and, when some sensualists had stopped before the booth, thinking perhaps a strip-tease act was due to take place inside, he started his patter. Pierrot stood stock still, dressed as a Persian.

At length the hall filled up, and the curtain rose on a sort of ironmongery. Pierrot stood in the midst of this, rooted to the spot. When the fakir made his entrance, Pierrot folded his arms and bowed low.

'I pulled that one off all right,' he thought. The other motioned to him. Pierrot, with an obsequious gesture, handed him a hatpin twelve inches long, which Crouia Bey stuck through his right cheek. The point came out of his mouth. At a second sign, Pierrot held out a new hatpin, with which Crouia Bey perforated his other cheek. A third pin was then stuck through the right cheek, and so on and so forth.

Absorbed in his work, Pierrot had not paid much attention to what became of the hatpins, but, about to proffer the sixth, he raised his eyes.

Through a fog he dimly perceived some species of steel barb emerging from the fakir's beard. He turned pale, watching the course of this latest hatpin. It was poised in the air and slowly, having pierced the outer skin, disappeared deep in the fakir's flesh. Pierrot looked on aghast, with eyes starting out of his head. Then the point of the pin reappeared between the fakir's lips. Pierrot could stand it no longer. Pierrot fainted.

A pandemonium of laughter broke out in the booth.

This is a section from *Pierrot Mon Ami*, the English title of which is *The Palace of Laughter*.

Jocelyn Brooke

THE SCAPEGOAT

(from a work in progress)

WAITING on the darkening platform, in the shrewd easterly wind, Gerald March slapped his riding-crop repeatedly, with angry violence, against his thighs; he was in an extremely bad temper. The wind was cold, the train late; a parcel which should have arrived, by rail, a week ago, had not come, or had been lost in transit. But these were mere straws, piled for good measure upon the heavier load which oppressed him.

He strode up and down, in a measured beat of a few yards, like a policeman: six feet four, and almost disproportionately broad, he made a commanding and rather impressive figure—or so he liked to believe, and in fact most people who didn't know him too well, would have agreed with him. At forty-five, he had kept the beefy youthfulness of an ex-rugger player; he was openly proud of the fact, and extremely sensitive about any reference to his age. At the same time he was secretly, unhappily aware of being past his prime: his body had begun to protest, at last, against a too-long-protracted boyishness; the greying hair proclaimed the fact to the world, and in private, before the mirror, the fold in the belly, the slackening pectoral muscle, told their tale.

Passing the cloakroom, he heard the porter (whom he had just scolded) enquiring about the parcel for 'the Colonel'. The courtesy-title pleased him: he had retired from the Army, with the rank of Major, two years before, when his father had died, and he had inherited what he commonly referred to as the 'estate'. Like his Colonel's rank, the estate was little more than a courtesy-title: his inheritance, apart from a not very valuable share in his grandfather's business, and a few rather dubious investments, consisted of a small converted farm-house, and a farm of two hundred acres which his father had bought on his retirement, and run as a hobby for a time: finally letting the land to a tenant, who had consistently mismanaged it for a number of years. But people still spoke of 'the Colonel's estate', much to Gerald's satisfaction. Accepted by what remained of the few county families in the district, but not especially popular with them, he was glad of such props to his social status. He had served with a good regiment, his family had been to the same public-school for two or three generations, but the fact remained, his grandfather had been in the wine-trade; they were not ' county ', and Gerald, whose brother-officers had mostly answered, if only approximately, to the coveted description, was extremely sensitive on the point.

He had resigned his commission with the intention of settling down as a country gentleman, and perhaps running the farm as a side-line like his father before him. As things turned out, however, the best he could hope for was to be a gentleman-farmer. He realized soon enough that his father's tenant had brought the farm near to ruin. Nothing, it appeared, but unlimited capital—or perhaps unlimited hard work—could save it. Lacking the capital, Gerald resigned himself to hard work. The tenant, lazy and a drunkard, was easily bought out; but the transaction was an expensive one, and after two years of unremitting labour, Gerald saw little prospect of realizing his ambition—which was to sell off the farm as soon as he could, and settle down, on the proceeds, to a life of modest (but gentlemanly) ease. He had even begun, lately, to regret leaving the Army, for with the likelihood of an imminent war, the prospects of promotion were brighter than for many years.

And now, to add to his misfortunes, his sister had died, and appointed him her son's guardian. Not that this was, financially, a disadvantage: Arabella had been fairly well-off, and her son's future was provided for. A sum had been laid aside to cover his school-fees and other expenses; the residue, at present held in trust, he would inherit when he came of age. Should he predecease his uncle—an unlikely event, though the boy was supposed to be delicate—the estate would revert to Gerald. In addition, Arabella had been generous, and her brother had received a legacy of a thousand pounds.

No, financially the situation was no worse: what irked him was the responsibility of making a home for the boy. Gerald, at forty-five, had a deep-rooted horror of being what he privately referred to as ' caught '. A bachelor, he had, for most of his life, successfully avoided entanglements, emotional or otherwise. He had been ' caught ' once, by the farm; and now he was caught again, doubly caught. He couldn't refuse the guardianship of Arabella's boy, and he was bound to make some sort of home for him. Not that he had been particularly attached to his sister; but he had a strong sense of family duty, and there seemed no way out of it. He had disapproved of Arabella's marriage in the first place; still more strongly had he disapproved of her upbringing of Duncan. The boy should have been sent to a proper prep. school, as a boarder, at the normal age: but Arabella would never hear of it. She had agreed, after much argument, to send him to a public-school (though she cherished a weakness for some place called Bedales): but

Gerald considered that the concession had come too late, and he had washed his hands of the affair. He could hardly foresee that Arabella would die when she did (though for that matter one might have expected something of the kind, with all that faith-healing nonsense); or that, dying, she would bequeath to himself the full weight of a responsibility which, even in a mitigated form, he had lately been careful to decline.

Still, the deed was done: he was ' caught '—properly caught. Anyway, Gerald reflected, we'll have to try and make a man of him; as far as the boy himself was concerned, it might be the making of him. He'd had too much of Arabella's silliness, no doubt. One might even manage to get him into Sandhurst.

At last the train pulled in, and Gerald searched the line of windows for the half-remembered face. Yes, there he was: carrot-haired, white-faced—not a bad-looking kid, but unhealthy. Looks like a girl, Gerald thought; and as he stepped forward to the carriage, he saw that the kid had obviously been crying. More soft-hearted than he liked to imagine, he felt a strong impulse of sympathy for the boy: after all, he had lost his mother. At the same time, mingled with his sympathy, he felt a peculiar disquiet, almost like a premonition of misfortune. Duncan's face (the train had stopped now) looked oddly insubstantial, ghost-like, in the uncertain light, filling Gerald with an obscure sense of complexity, a feeling that the situation was less simple than it seemed. . . . Ridiculous, he thought, brushing the idea aside; I'm getting ' nervy '. Must be all the war-talk you heard nowadays: the ' war of nerves ' as they called it.

As Duncan stepped on to the platform, Gerald greeted him with genial affection.

' Hullo, kiddo,' he said. ' Glad to see you. I've got the old bus outside. We'll just collect your luggage, shall we?' Grasping the boy's arm, he hurried him along towards the luggage-van.

Huddled beside his uncle in the front of the battered, mud-stained Morris, Duncan hardly replied to Gerald's kindly-meant questions and remarks. The sense of danger which had assailed him, as the train pulled in, persisted: and as each new impression impinged on his senses, he felt more acutely than ever that he had arrived in an alien land. In his nostrils, the smell of wet mackintosh and leather mingled with the alkaline tang of the sea, impressing him afresh with strangeness. The bourgeois seaside-town, sliding past in the thickening dusk, seemed unfriendly: solid, sham-Georgian houses behind laurels, with spiky gates. As they passed through the poorer quarter, a child ran across the street, and, when Gerald slammed the brakes on, a woman screamed at them angrily, and a group of soldiers, standing at the corner, laughed and shouted obscenities.

Meanwhile Gerald kept up a one-sided, rather gusty conversation: 'Hope you'll settle down all right—not what you've been used to, exactly, of course; but if you like the country, and country sort of things, you'll be O.K. . . . 'Fraid you'll have to rather make your own amusements . . . fact is, I'm hellish busy at the moment . . . bitten off more than I can chew . . . can't afford to take on any more labour. . . . Done any riding? You ought to take to it—we can fix you up with something. . . . There, we're out of that blasted town. This is Gibbet Hill—used to be a gibbet here somewhere. . . . You'll be able to see the house in a sec.'

The car breasted a steep flank of down, treeless, sharp-edged against the western sky. Presently the road dipped again, revealing a more domesticated country of small valleys and wooded hills.

'Look—you can see the house now: those lights, below there.'

Dimly, lights showed in the valley, beneath a humped mass of woodland. The house appeared in vague outline; at the side, a short distance from the house itself, stood a group of extraordinary shapes; to Duncan they seemed like the figures of enormous women, in cowled headdresses, overtopping the house: figures of a dream, gigantic and menacing.

'What are those—those . . .' surely they must be buildings after all—'those chimney-things?' Duncan asked.

'Oh, the oast-houses. I suppose you don't get 'em in your part of the country. For drying hops. Don't go in for hops much, myself— not enough land to spare. The oasts date from when the farm was a much bigger concern. . . . No, fruit's more in my line: I want to go in for it in a big way.'

At last the car pulled up before the house. Little could be seen of it in the darkness: a row of gables appeared indistinctly against the sky, suggesting the form of an enormous bat's wing. Duncan followed his uncle through the open door. Sims, Gerald's ex-soldier-servant, carried in the luggage. A dourly good-looking man, he smiled in a rather guarded way at Duncan.

'He's my main stand-by,' Gerald explained. 'Does most of the house-work, cooks, does any odd job. I haven't much use for women about the place, myself. We have to have a daily girl from the village, but you can't get 'em to sleep in nowadays.'

The door led into an entrance-hall which apparently included sitting-room and dining-room. A fire of oak-boughs burnt sulkily in the grate, and a table was laid for a meal. Gerald's father had bought the house after his wife's death, and since the Marches had been in possession, it had been exclusively a house of men. No feminine elegancies relieved the austere masculinity of the room. There were leather chairs, pipe-racks, ash-trays, foxes' masks, an assortment of horns: the only pictures were a few sporting prints and football groups. Half-consciously Duncan found himself looking for a single homely touch—flowers, loose-covers, cushions, anything to soften the room's austerity—but found none. Gerald had shared with his father a taste for masculine comfort, without frills; it would no more have occurred to him (for instance) to have flowers in a room, than to use scent, or to have his nails manicured.

Duncan, sorting out his baggage, looked up questioningly at his uncle. He was impressed again, as he had been at the station, by his enormous size: the room was a large one, but scarcely seemed big enough to contain its owner with comfort.

Gerald grinned amiably.

'I expect you're hungry,' he said. 'I'll show you up to your room, and then we'll feed.'

His voice and manner were purely friendly, yet Duncan still had a disquieting sense of lurking danger. Out of the corner of his eye, as he bent over the suitcases, he studied Gerald's face. Broad, healthily tanned, of a tough, leathery texture, there was nothing extraordinary about it. When he smiled, his lips opened squarely, like a trapdoor, beneath the small bristly moustache, revealing a set of sound, regular teeth. His thick, darkish hair, beginning to turn grey, was cropped extremely short at the back and sides, and this gave his large, well-shaped head a curiously naked appearance.

'Ready? Come on then, we'll go up. You're sleeping in what used to be my dressing-room. We thought it'd be less lonely for you there at first.'

It was, as a matter of fact, Arabella's housekeeper who had thought it would be 'less lonely'; she had taken Gerald aside after the funeral, and spoken of Duncan's 'nerves'. 'He's hardly used to sleeping quite alone,' she had explained. 'Ours is a small house, and he's always been within call. He's better now than he used to be, but seeing as he's going to a strange house, if you could put him somewhere near you. . . .' And Gerald, who privately thought that 'nerves' were all rot in a boy of thirteen, had obediently had a bed made up in the small room leading out of his own bedroom.

'Hope you'll be comfortable. . . . Shouldn't bother to unpack much tonight. . . . The bathroom's just across the passage—the rear's next door. Come down when you're ready, and I'll tell Sims to buck up with the supper.'

The small room was bare as a monk's cell: a bed, a chair, a bedside-table, nothing else. Duncan unpacked a few necessities, and went to have a wash. He moved with a careful deliberation, trying to quell the disturbance in his mind. But it was as though a crowd of people surrounded him, all giving him contradictory advice. The most trivial action was fraught with indecision. He took up a toothbrush to brush his hair, the soap slipped from his hand and could not be found, the towel fell into the basin.

At last, wearily, he went to the window and looked out. Very faintly the humped wood showed against the sky. A light gleamed dimly from some cottage immediately opposite. As he stood, looking out, he fancied that he heard a curious singing noise, an indeterminate droning like the noise in a sea-shell. Probably it was some trick of the wind, or merely that he was extremely tired. . . . He turned from the window, and reluctantly prepared to join his uncle. Passing through the large bedroom, he recognized the heavy, valuable-looking toilet articles—the razor-strop, boot-trees, silver brushes. A camel-hair dressing-gown hung over a chair, and a pair of rather old-fashioned ' frogged ' pyjamas was laid out ready for the night. On the wall hung several regimental groups: one included Gerald, in rugger-kit, glowering angrily at the camera. Duncan remembered that he had once played rugger for the Army.

He turned away, rather hopelessly, and, sick with fatigue and nostalgia, a stranger in enemy country, made his way slowly downstairs.

Duncan woke early the next morning. It was still dark, but he could hear his uncle moving about next door. Presently Gerald looked in, fully-dressed. To Duncan, dozing off again, he appeared like a sudden portent, disturbing as a bugle-blast. Fresh from his bath, wearing whipcord riding-breeches and a rough tweed coat, he exhaled an overmastering, a rather monstrous vitality. Liable, by nature, to be bad-tempered before breakfast, his face was sullen, and when he spoke he sounded stern almost to the point of anger, though his words were friendly enough.

' Awake already? Don't hurry to get up. I have to turn out early, to see to things . . . Sims'll call you later. I've told him to run you a bath. I have a cold one myself, but no doubt you're used to a hot one. See you at breakfast.'

He disappeared abruptly, and Duncan, with an immense relief, pulled the clothes over his head and drew his knees up to his chin, as though by concealing himself and making himself as small as possible, he could exclude the new life which, like a raw, unaccustomed climate, awaited him outside the small private kingdom of his bed.

Drowsily, but with a deliberate effort to escape from the imminence of what lay before him, he urged himself further and further into the remote territories of his own imagination, till at last he reached the innermost sanctuary, the inviolable province of his most private phantasy.

This ultramontane country, visited irregularly, was of a variable land-scape, but its most usual aspect was that of a South-Sea island, blessed with perpetual fine weather, and having a sandy beach, a lagoon, a roughly-built log-cabin—all the paraphernalia, in fact, of *Coral Island* (which was Duncan's favourite book, except for *Mr. Tod*); but with this advantage, that the population was of his own choosing. Or so, at least, he had always imagined; on his last visit, the inhabitants had consisted of the head-boy at his day-school, and—a recent immigrant —one of the younger masters from his public-school. This morning, however, to his surprise, who should be waiting for him on the shore of the island but his uncle: attired, rather unsuitably, in rugger-kit, and glaring sullenly before him as he had glared from the photograph in the bedroom. Duncan saluted him, gravely: once ashore on the island, his right to be there could not be questioned. His presence was in itself a passport; he would remain there for as long as he chose, a naturalized citizen of a world existing beyond the bounds of time and space.

Sims' voice roused Duncan, an hour later, from a half-sleep, proffering a hot bath. Once out of bed, a curious deliberate valour took possession of him. He felt once more, as he had felt in the train, a determination to excel, to come to terms with this naked, unfamiliar life. On his way through his uncle's room, he paused to look at the photograph of the rugger-group. Gerald, his immense thighs bulging from exiguous shorts, frowned back at him sternly and compellingly. Tomorrow, Duncan decided, he would get up early and have a cold bath; probably he would learn to ride, too, as his uncle had suggested. . . .

In the bathroom, he observed Gerald's razor, which lay on the window-ledge: a cut-throat of old-fashioned pattern. Curiously, he picked it up: it slipped in his hand, and he cut himself slightly. The bright blood, splashing suddenly on the white enamelled basin, startled him. A drop had fallen on the blade of the razor, and he was about to wipe it off, but suddenly decided to leave it: he could not have explained why, but the decision was accompanied by a curious feeling of pleasure.

Back in his room, he looked out at the bright, wintry morning. The woods lay still and silent in the early sun. Vaguely Duncan found him-self looking for the house or cottage whose light he had seen the night before: it should have been exactly opposite his window, on the steepest part of the hillside. No house, however, was visible. The wood was thin at that point, and any building, however small, must have shown up clearly. Surprised, he turned away and began to dress.

At breakfast, Duncan asked his uncle about the light in the wood: the absence of any obvious explanation had set up a kind of reverberation of anxiety in his mind. Gerald, when he heard the question, shot a curious look at him: for a moment, it almost seemed as if he were embarrassed.

'There's no house there—on the hillside. Nearest one's the keeper's cottage, and that's a couple of miles away. . . . Nobody would be out in the wood at that time of night, unless it was a poacher—and a poacher would hardly carry a light. No—you must have been seeing things.' He laughed, and his expression was so frank and normal, that Duncan mentally discounted what had seemed his 'embarrassment' of a moment before. He must, he realized, have been mistaken: there was something about Gerald's manner, he thought, which made it easy to misunderstand him.

After breakfast, Gerald suggested a tour of the farm. 'Might as well get the lie of the land,' he said. Secretly, Gerald was rather looking forward to showing off the farm to someone who would not be too critical.

In front of the house were the relics of a garden: a square of neglected lawn, surrounded by unweeded flower-beds and unpruned rambler-roses.

'No time for flower-gardening,' Gerald explained. 'You might take a turn at it, if you care for that sort of thing.'

They paused to look up at the house: faced with grey cement, it appeared an undistinguished, mid-Victorian structure, decent and homely, but lacking in charm.

'Parts of it are old, though you'd not think it. Fourteenth century. It's all been built round at different times. They say the name—Friarsholt—has something to do with an abbey or priory or something that lay just near. I've never been into all that myself. No time. The pater had some odd sort of theories. Interested in history and all that. I've never had time for it.'

Gerald laughed, but Duncan had an odd impression that he was dropping the subject rather quickly. For a moment, his face wore the expression which Duncan had noticed—or thought he had noticed—when he mentioned the mysterious light.

The morning was cold and clear, with a high pale sky. Twigs and leaves were fledged with rime, and ice lay thinly in the cart-tracks and puddles. Beyond the garden, fields fell away to the left: to the right, a track bordered by a tall hedge, interspersed with hollies and yew-trees, led up the hillside to where the woods began. Far away, at the highest point on the skyline, the woods were topped by what appeared to be a pointed white cap, like a mushroom.

'Oh, that's the old water-tower,' Gerald explained, when questioned, 'Here are the cowsheds, you see. Still in need of repair, I'm afraid. The cowman's O.K., but he's always telling me how the other bloke ran things. Conservative lot, the farm people round here. I think we'll go round by Forty Acres—I want to have a look at that wheat Jarvis was talking about. And then you'll be able to see where I want to plant out my new orchards. It's time that Wychwood field was grassed down, too—it's been no bloody good since I can remember.'

Duncan listened with intense concentration, following at his uncle's side. They made a complete tour of the farm, Gerald talking without interruption, referring constantly to people, things and places of which Duncan could obviously never have heard. After two hours of it, he had talked himself into a mood of extraordinary joviality. His mood infected Duncan, who was flattered at being talked to as a grown-up and an equal; moreover, having habituated himself, since his mother's death to expect the worst of his uncle, he was apt to overvalue the least show of kindness or flattery, construing it as a sign of genuine friendship, even of love. And now that Gerald was an inhabitant of the Island, he would have been, in any case, predisposed in his favour.

Walking round the farm, listening to the endless flow of his uncle's talk, Duncan felt a renewal of his determination to come to terms with this alien yet exciting world of which Gerald, with his bouncing athleticism, was the despotic and exclusive ruler. He recognized in himself the first symptoms of one of his obsessional attachments: but in this case, the affair promised to be on an altogether larger scale. It was as though his previous ' crazes ', as his mother used to call them, had been the preparatory stages in a process which was now nearing its logical conclusion. The ferrets, the fireworks, the rabbit-scutted soldiers in the shrubbery, had been, as it were, a series of rehearsals, incomplete or abortive attempts at the real thing. The process had begun, he realized, when he went to school last September; but it was Gerald's presence on the ' Island ' that had finally revealed the course which he was destined to take.

In the light of his new knowledge, the details of the farm-work, as Gerald explained them, took on a magical significance: Gerald's whole conversation, in fact, was a perpetual incantation, binding him ever more securely in his new and self-imposed captivity: a captivity which, though he desired it and sought to hasten its completion, was yet fraught with a strange dread, a prescience of unimaginable danger.

Gerald continued to chatter amiably. The fact was, he had been suffering lately from the lack of a good listener. Men of his own class were few in the district, and those who would listen to him without interruption, fewer still. Gerald seldom went far afield in search of society; once a month or so he would spend a week-end in London, but even in London he had lost touch with many of his friends. Duncan, in fact, was the first person he had been able to talk to for a considerable time who possessed the twin advantages of not being a farm-hand or a servant, and not interrupting.

At the stables, Duncan was given a break. The groom was a talkative man, and endlessly anxious to discuss the foibles of Blackshirt, Gerald's expensive and seldom-used hunter. Gerald was willing enough to talk horses, and soon he and the groom were deep in technicalities. At one point, their voices sank almost to a whisper, and Gerald suddenly interrupted himself to fling a question at Duncan.

'You'd like to take up riding, wouldn't you?' he asked.

'I'd love to,' Duncan replied, without hesitation: secretly alarmed, but strong in his new determination.

The conversation in the stable proceeded in undertones, Duncan waiting in the doorway. Presently Gerald turned away, with a final word to the groom, and rejoined his nephew.

'I've got a few jobs to do indoors, now,' he said. 'D'you think you can amuse yourself till lunch-time? Go anywhere you like, you know. Any ideas you get—anything you want to do, just let's hear about it.' Grinning good-temperedly, he walked away towards the house.

Left alone, Duncan felt a sudden sinking of the heart. A moment before, his whole being had been concentrated, with a conscious and laborious marshalling of his faculties, upon the task of appearing worthy in his uncle's eyes. Now, with Gerald's departure, the impulsion which had keyed him up, for the past two hours, to an unaccustomed alertness, subsided abruptly. With a sudden backwash of emotion, he knew only that he had lost his mother and his home, and that he was in a strange country, afraid and without protection.

The sky had become overcast, with a thin luminous film of cloud obscuring the sun. Duncan mooched unhappily round the derelict garden, and leaned over the front gate. He would have liked to go for a walk, but the country seemed unfriendly and forbidding. The silent brown mass of the wood impended heavily upon the house, watchful and menacing; there was about it something ancient and still untamed: one could imagine, in some future time, the forests creeping back gradually to engulf the farm-lands, the scattered houses overgrown and subsiding, the whole countryside reverting, at last, to the old wealden jungle. To Duncan, the most innocent objects—a spade stuck in a flowerbed, a fallen, moss-grown garden-urn, the dried seed-capsules of a delphinium—were suddenly impregnated with a sense of fatality: their silent, reticent forms seemed to be signalling a note of warning. To westward, on the skyline above the woods, the white cap of the water-tower beckoned with an equivocal invitation, promising he knew not what consummation of happiness.

In the hedge by the gate, a few spindle-berries lingered—it had been a mild autumn—wrinkled and withering, the orange seeds clinging precariously to their puce-coloured envelopes. Tears stung Duncan's eyes, as he remembered that his mother had loved them. Under the hedge, nearby, some woolly pink heads of the winter-butterbur were showing through a carpet of dead leaves. Stooping to pick one, he inhaled the familiar heliotrope scent, and a fresh spasm of tears crumpled his face.

He leaned over the gate, his eyes fixed on the distant water-tower. Presently a sound of heavy, regular footsteps in the road distracted him. A column of soldiers was coming round the corner: one of the battalions in training at the neighbouring barracks. Weighed down with the cumbrous webbing-equipment, sweating in spite of the cold, their raw, meat-red faces surly beneath steel-helmets, they passed heavily down the narrow lane. To Duncan, the silent, red-faced men seemed an integral part of the landscape, the indigenous fauna of an unexplored, unfriendly country. From where he stood, within a yard of the marching column, he could flair the faint whiff of sweat and stale urine which came off their muffled, constricted bodies: an animal, foxy scent, suggesting a way of life remote and primitive, conditioned by some cruel Mithraic discipline. The sight and smell of them affected Duncan with a lively and personal distaste, like the flavour of onions, which he detested. Yet their alien presence constituted a kind of challenge to the boy's new-found resolutions. Watching the column out of sight, he felt his primary disgust modulated, in some remote cavern of his mind, into a peculiar and inadmissible pleasure.

Presently he summoned the courage to walk out of the gate. Once outside, he crossed the road without further hesitation, and began to walk up the track towards the woods. A light wind had risen, rattling softly in the leaves of the hollies which stood out blankly, like dark, glistening fires, against the neutral-tinted landscape. Otherwise, the country seemed extraordinarily silent. Soon the path entered the wood, leading straight ahead through thickets of brown, sodden bracken. A pheasant shouted discordantly in the undergrowth, close at hand, startling the heavy woodland silence, which, after this brief disturbance, immediately descended again, seeming more intense than before.

Duncan walked on for some minutes, then, as a sudden idea struck him, branched off to the right, between the close-growing hazels. It would be about here, he decided, that he had seen the mysterious light the evening before. . . . He searched for some minutes, expecting to come upon a pile of ashes and charred sticks, or perhaps (in spite of what his uncle had said) some small hut or cabin. There were, however, no signs of any human visitor, except for an empty cartridge-case, which Duncan absently picked up and stuffed in his pocket. A bleached rabbit-skull also caught his attention, and this, too, he collected.

Returning to the path, he continued further into the wood, which continued monotonously on either side: hazel-thickets scattered with oaks or Spanish chestnuts. He scarcely knew how long he had been walking, when the path took a sudden turn, and the wood—or at least his part of it—came to an end. Climbing a hurdle which barred the path's end, he found himself in a sloping field, surrounded on three sides by woodland, and on the fourth dipping abruptly to a winding valley, beyond which more woods fringed the skyline.

As he stood at the field's edge, wondering which way to go, he saw a human figure emerge from the wood close by. It was an old man —immensely old, with a patriarchal beard, his limbs twisted by rheumatism: probably some woodman or casual labourer from a neighbouring farm. He approached Duncan, and touched his cap.

' Mornin', sir. Nice mornin'.'

He stood there, in no hurry to move on, it seemed: not looking at Duncan, but gazing across the field towards the valley.

' It's a bad place,' he muttered, more to himself than to the boy.

' Bad? ' Duncan queried.

The old man turned round, half-surprised at being overheard.

' Yes, a bad place. That there field—nought'd ever grow in 'er. They ploughed 'er up in the war, but it's bad land, no good to nobody. I could've told 'em, and saved 'em the trouble. I mind me grandfather sayin' it was a bad place: you couldn't get him to set foot on it, even.' The old man paused, and shook his head.

Duncan, looking across the field, noticed for the first time, about fifty yards away, a curious structure: two roughly-shaped stones standing upright, with another flattened stone lying horizontally across their summits. The whole was about ten feet tall. Duncan remembered pictures of Stonehenge, and supposed that this, too, was some pre-historic monument.

The old man had followed his eyes, and, as though to himself, muttered something indistinctly about ' Them stones '. He remained there, silent, for a few minutes longer. Then, as though his train of thought had come full circle, he repeated his original remark: ' It's a bad place.' Presently, with a polite ' good-morning ', he shambled off towards the path.

Curious to examine the stones, Duncan walked across the field towards them. The ground was rough, pitted with rabbit-holes, and clothed with the coarse, tufted taw-grass. Clumps of squalid, withering rag-wort, lingering in late bloom, made patches of faded yellow. A stunted thornbush grew near the stones, bent level with the ground by the south-west winds.

A few yards from the stones, Duncan stumbled over a rabbit-hole, and just saved himself from falling flat on his face. At his feet lay the remains of a dead sheep, far gone in rottenness. A gaping rent in the flesh revealed a pullulating mass of fat, whitish maggots.

Duncan started away, overcome by a sudden and extreme nausea. Turning in his tracks, he stumbled back towards the homeward path. The old man's words seemed to him invested with a new and sinister significance: 'It's a bad place.' As he reached the hurdle, he became suddenly aware of a confused noise; still preoccupied with the horrible thing in the field, his brain worked slowly, and he was only just in time to leap to safety as Gerald, galloping up the path on Blackshirt, cleared the hurdle and landed in the field.

Seeing his nephew, Gerald looked completely dumbfounded. His face went blank, his eyes gleaming darkly with a kind of angry bewilderment.

'What the devil are you doing here?' he shouted.

Duncan felt his mind swoon into an abyss of pure terror. It was true, he had nearly been ridden down; but Gerald's tone and expression, his white-faced, burning anger, had a quality of terrifying irrelevance. To say the least, his violent outburst seemed wildly out of proportion to any perceptible cause; and coming after the encounter with the dead sheep, seemed to Duncan in some mysterious way connected with it, so that the vision of the rotted carcase, with its obscene swarm of maggots, recurred in all its horror, haloed, as it were, with the fiery aura of his uncle's meaningless fury.

'Why—what . . .' Duncan stammered. 'I'm sorry I was in the way. I didn't . . .'

'Oh, all right, no offence.' Gerald grinned, suddenly normal again. 'You only startled me, rather, popping up like that.' He paused. Then he made a curious remark: 'I suppose you had to come here sooner or later.' The words were uttered so low that Duncan, mistrusting his ears, asked: 'What did you say?'

'Nothing. . . . What?' Gerald looked suddenly startled, as though roused from some private imagining.

'I thought you said something—I couldn't catch.'

'No—I don't know. Forget now what I *did* say.' He grinned again, all friendly. 'Been looking at the old Druids' stones, eh? There's some old what-do-you-call-'ems, too, hereabouts—tumuli. Tombs of Danes or Saxons or something. Yes, there they are . . .' he pointed with his crop to an opening in the wood, where three mounds, clothed with ivy and withering dogs'-mercury, rose from the level, leafy floor.

Duncan looked, without much interest, at the tombs; he was anxious to get away from the place. He suddenly noticed that the water-tower was visible again, dominating the wooded horizon.

'How far is it to the water-tower?' he asked his uncle.

Gerald looked dubious.

'Oh—I should say three or four miles—not much more.' He stared, consideringly, across the wooded, hilly landscape. The sunlight was now entirely obscured by thickening clouds: the country seemed to have gone dead, brooding in a silent, malevolent dream. Duncan, watching his uncle, half-fearing a fresh outburst, felt himself stiffening to withstand the assault of terror. Danger flickered over the woods like lightning. It was a bad place.

'Could I go there sometime—to the water-tower?' Duncan asked, nervously. He didn't want to pursue the subject, yet felt a curious compulsion to do so. He waited, uneasily, possessed by an excruciating need to make water.

'To the water-tower?' Gerald looked vague: he seemed almost to have forgotten the topic, already. Suddenly he stared full in Duncan's face, and the boy was aware once more of something equivocal in his expression: as though he were embarrassed or ashamed. Duncan dropped his eyes.

'I only wondered . . .' he muttered.

'Oh, yes, you could go, I suppose. . . .' Gerald spoke without much interest, wheeling his horse round towards the path. He paused. 'But I don't know that I should bother. I mean, there's nothing to go there for—just an old tower.'

'I only thought perhaps . . .'

'Oh, yes, go if you want to.' Gerald seemed suddenly annoyed, and Duncan flinched, cursing his own importunity. 'Time enough to think about that later,' Gerald added, with another sudden switch to joviality. 'At the moment it's time we were getting back to lunch. D'you mind pulling the hurdle aside? I'm not going to take him over this time.'

Duncan paused, when the horse had passed through, to urinate at the side of the path. He was oddly embarrassed by his uncle's presence, and it was some minutes before he turned to accompany Gerald down the track. On horseback, Gerald seemed more than ever monumental: he rode superbly, moulded like a centaur to the horse's body. His whole figure alert, the muscles flexed, he gave a curious impression of being too big for his clothes, as if his enormous body resented the impediment of whipcord and tweed.

Half-fearful, half-admiring, Duncan trotted at his side. A little way down the path, Gerald suddenly pulled up his horse.

'Look there!' He pointed upwards into the overhanging branches of a tree. Duncan saw an orbicular mass of green twigs—perhaps a rook's nest? He looked again.

'Why, it's mistletoe,' he said. 'I never noticed it.'

'We'd better get some for Christmas,' Gerald suggested. 'Here, hold Blackshirt—it's all right, he won't bite you.' With the agility of a circus-rider, he stood up on the saddle, and swung himself bodily on to the branch, sitting it astride. It was a considerable feat for a man of forty-five. Duncan watched him admiringly, as he cut off the mistletoe with a jack-knife, flung it on to the path, and then lowered himself, confidently, on to the saddle again.

Duncan handed him up the mistletoe; he took it, glanced at it with an expression of pleasure, then handed it back: presenting it to his nephew with an oddly eager, rather ceremonious air.

'Thank you very much,' the boy murmured politely.

There was something strangely ceremonial about the whole incident: it was as though it were part of some ritual. Duncan was vaguely puzzled: Gerald's air, as he handed him the mistletoe, was oddly apologetic: the expression of one who makes an inadequate amends for some injury. The moment passed: Gerald laughed—rather as one who 'laughs off' some unpleasant or embarrassing episode.

'I don't know who you'll find to kiss under it,' he chuckled. 'We don't run to pretty girls much, here.'

Duncan laughed politely; but a curious idea was forming at the back of his mind. There were, it seemed to him, two Uncle Geralds: the normal, jovial everyday personality, and the other—secret, menacing, given to sudden strange embarrassments and bursts of anger.

The 'normal' Gerald was uppermost at the moment. He chatted and joked in his facile, amiable strain all the way back to the house. As before, Duncan found this attitude flattering, and he found it easy to forget, while Gerald's mood lasted, that other and darker aspect of his uncle which existed, so it seemed, behind the bluff, benevolent façade.